Mexico Urbanization Review

DIRECTIONS IN DEVELOPMENT
Countries and Regions

Mexico Urbanization Review

Managing Spatial Growth for Productive and Livable Cities in Mexico

Yoonhee Kim and Bontje Zangerling, Editors

WORLD BANK GROUP

Contents

Boxes

Figures

Tables

Acknowledgments

This study was conducted by a team led by Yoonhee Kim (Senior Urban Economist, Social, Urban, Rural, and Resilience Global Practice—GSURR) that included Bontje Zangerling (Urban Specialist, GSURR), Angélica Núñez del Campo (Senior Urban Specialist, GSURR), Nancy Lozano-Gracia (Senior Economist, GSURR), Andrea Betancourt (Consultant, GSURR), Bernadette Baird-Zars (Consultant, GSURR), and Ondina Francisca Rocca (Consultant, GSURR). The study draws extensively on background consultant reports and analytical inputs prepared by Paavo Monkkonen (Assistant Professor of Urban Planning at the Luskin School of Public Affairs, University of California, Los Angeles—UCLA), Rafael Garduño (Research Professor, Centro de Investigación y Docencia Económicas—CIDE), and Laura Atuesta (Visiting Assistant Professor, CIDE). In addition, Nicole Walter (Research Assistant, ULCA), María del Pilar Fuerte Celis (Independent Consultant), and Gabriel Parada Colin (CIDE) provided various analytical support and assistance to the study. The team benefitted from the excellent guidance and constructive feedback from Catalina Marulanda (Lead Urban Specialist, GSURR), Alexandra Ortiz (Program Leader, Mexico and Colombia Country Management Unit—LCC1C), and Anna Wellenstein (Former Practice Manager and Practice Director, GSURR). The team also benefitted from the superb support of Ana F. Daza (Program Assistant, GSURR), Diana Gabriela Jimenez Cruz (Program Assistant, LCC1C), and Beatriz Eugenia Gomez Villasenor (Temporary, LCC1C). The executive summary was edited by Communications Development Incorporated.

The study was carried out with the active involvement of government counterparts led by Rosario Robles, Secretary for Agrarian, Land, and Urban Development (*Secretaria de Desarrollo Agrario, Territorial y Urbano*, SEDATU) and included the participation of many of her staff. The report also benefitted from technical discussions with the directors and staff from other housing agencies, including CONAVI (National Housing Commission, *Comisión Nacional de Vivienda*), INFONAVIT (Federal Institute for Workers' Housing, *Instituto del Fondo Nacional de la Vivienda para los Trabajadores*), SHF (Federal Mortgage Society, *Socieded Hipotecaria Federal*), and FOVISSSTE (Housing Fund of the Social Security and Services Institute for State Workers, *Fondo de la Vivienda del Instituto de Seguridad y Servicios Sociales de los Trabajadores del Estado*). The support of these officials is gratefully acknowledged.

The team received valuable comments from the following peer reviewers at the project concept note, quality enhancement review, and decision review stages: Somik Lall (Lead Urban Economist, GSURR), Peter D. Ellis (Lead Urban Economist, GSURR), and Austin Francis Louis Kilroy (Private Sector Development Specialist, Trade and Competitiveness Global Practice—GTCDR).

In preparing the report, the team is grateful for the guidance from senior management of the World Bank's Social, Urban, Rural, and Resilience Global Practice, notably Senior Director Ede Jorge Ijjasz-Vasquez and former Director Marisela Muñoz. In addition, the team is thankful for the support received from the Country Management team, particularly, Country Director for Mexico Gerardo M. Corrochano and former Country Director Gloria M. Grandolini. The team received generous support from the World Bank Multi-Donor Trust Fund for Sustainable Urbanization, whose financial contribution constituted an important part of the report.

Executive Summary: Managing Spatial Growth for Productive and Livable Cities in Mexico

Urbanization in Mexico, as in other countries around the world, has been associated with increased prosperity and reduced poverty. It has also gone hand in hand with economic growth. About 77 percent of the country's population lived in urban areas in 2010, and 87 percent of its gross value added (GVA) was produced in cities with populations over 100,000. The average real household labor income in cities with more than 100,000 inhabitants increased across all cities between 1990 and 2010. The increase was sharpest in big cities, where average household income nearly quadrupled between 1990 and 2010. Meanwhile, income poverty fell across all city groups, with the largest reductions in medium cities.

Cities are engines of economic growth that foster high value-added activities and innovation. Economic innovation and productivity in firms often grow most easily in dense and connected urban environments, where labor, knowledge, and new ideas are just a few minutes away. And those new sectors that are most likely to tap into growing global markets often incubate and flourish best in cities. Well-functioning cities connect jobs and markets, providing urban amenities and livable space conducive to high value-added economic activities. High value-added firms thrive in large urban centers where they can learn from many other types of high value-added firms. Proximity and agglomeration allow ideas to spread and grow among people.

Distant, Dispersed, and Disconnected Spatial Growth in Mexican Cities

Despite impressive economic growth and prosperity, cities in Mexico do not seem to have fully captured the benefits from agglomeration, in part because of the way most Mexican cities expanded in the past. One of the key challenges facing many Mexican cities has been the rapid and uncoordinated growth of urban footprints, characterized as *distant*, *dispersed*, and *disconnected*. Over the past 30 years, the built-up areas of Mexican cities expanded sevenfold and the urbanized areas of the 11 biggest metropolitan cities ninefold. This horizontal expansion has been driven mainly by large single-use housing developments on the outskirts of cities. The urban growth has largely happened unplanned and has been connected to the fissure between new developments and the provision of educational and health facilities, infrastructure, connectivity, and proximity of sources of employment. The way Mexican cities grew in the past has underused the cities' potential to boost economic growth and foster social inclusion and livability.

The construction boom and expansion of housing finance, coupled with the absence of effective urban planning, are connected to the uncoordinated sprawl of Mexican cities. The reform of housing policies and expansion in the Federal Institute for Workers' Housing (*Instituto del Fondo Nacional de la Vivienda para los Trabajadores*, INFONAVIT), the largest source of loans in Mexico and Latin America, contributed to improving the access to housing for the poor since the early 2000s.[1] However, expansion toward the periphery in the past has overwhelmingly occurred without clearly demarcated planning guidelines, boundaries for growth, and zoning. The peri-urban location of housing developments and the lack of supporting infrastructure and urban amenities have created important economic and social consequences in Mexican cities. Alerted by this uncoordinated urban sprawl, Mexican policy makers included compact development and densification of cities as key goals in the national urban policy framework launched in 2013. An ambitious urban policy agenda now aims to control urban expansion and promote more productive and livable inclusive cities.

Objective and Scope of the Urbanization Review

In response to the government's policy priorities, this Urbanization Review (UR) sets out to provide an analytical basis to understand how well-managed spatial growth can further contribute to unlocking the gains from urbanization. More specifically, the UR responds to the questions of: (i) what have been the patterns of spatial expansion within Mexican cities; (ii) what have been the associated economic, social, and fiscal implications; (iii) what are the underlying policy and institutional drivers for the spatial expansion; and (iv) what are the key policy messages and recommendations to enhance spatial growth of the cities. To this end, the report first analyzes the spatial development patterns of Mexican cities by creating a set of spatial indexes for the 100 largest cities and reviews the main policy shortcomings that have resulted in uncoordinated urban expansion. It also reviews the overall performance and remaining challenges for Mexican cities to drive the transition into a high-income country and examines how recent urban spatial growth has affected economic performance and livability of Mexican cities. Based on the analysis, it offers adjustment to policy framework and instruments to support more sustainable spatial development and to make Mexican cities become more productive and inclusive.

The analysis of the UR shows that well-managed spatial growth could support realizing inclusive and productive potentials of Mexican cities. In addition, urban form is multifaceted and multidimensional; it requires more granulated analysis at the local level in order to understand the dynamics of spatial patterns and to devise the right policy measures. The government's policy response to the uncoordinated urban growth has been largely through housing policies and focusing on controlling urban expansion. Housing policies can certainly promote dense, connected, and coordinated growth. However, housing policy alone will not be enough to address the challenges that Mexican cities face to contribute to economic growth and inclusiveness. Instead, a well-coordinated urban policy and instruments at the national level that take into account the multifaceted nature and implications of urban form are needed to achieve well-managed urban growth. In addition, the current urban policy can benefit from moving away from its density-driven focus on controlling urban expansion and strengthening local-level planning and taking into account multifaceted urban form in policy design.

Box ES.1 Mexico Has a Consolidated System of Cities that Is Fairly Balanced across Urban Agglomeration of All Sizes

In 2010, more than 72 percent of Mexicans lived in the country's 384 cities that have more than 15,000 inhabitants. The Mexico City Metropolitan Area (MCMA), with a quarter of the urban population in 2010 (20.1 million residents), is by far the biggest urban agglomeration in the country and the biggest in Latin America. However, large cities with between 1 and 10 million inhabitants, gaining in importance over the past decade, are now home to 26 percent of the country's urban population. Another 20 percent of urban residents live in medium-size cities and 17 percent in small cities. The 289 small towns with fewer than 100,000 inhabitants host only 12 percent (map BES.1.1).

Map BES.1.1 System of Cities in Mexico

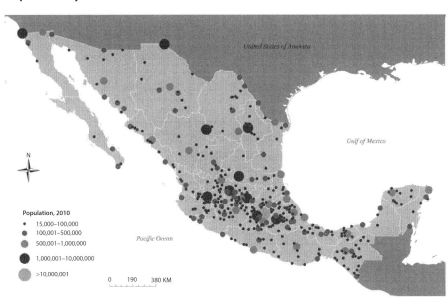

Source: World Bank analysis based on data from the Secretariat of Social Development (*Secretariat de Desarrollo Social*, SEDESOL).

Unlocking the Economic Potentials of Mexican Cities

Understanding how peri-urban expansion dampens economic potentials can redirect policies to capitalize on the benefits from agglomeration economies in Mexico. How cities grow, expand infrastructure and connectivity, and unlock agglomeration economies can shape their productive potential. Urban form lays the groundwork for cities to fulfill economic functions. Spatial dynamics of cities influence the distance between people and employment and can also affect the ability of people to connect with one another and the government's capacity to equip properly an entire urban area with infrastructure and services. Firms choose to settle in particular locations considering aspects such as land prices, access to workers, and transport costs. Firms may have reduced access to workers with specific skill sets in sprawling cities, in particular if these suffer from lagging transportation services, long commuting times, congestion, and high transportation costs. In addition, long distances between homes and jobs in the absence of adequate connective infrastructure can prevent workers from accessing suitable jobs and interacting with other skilled workers.

Uncoordinated urban growth in Mexican cities widened the distance between jobs and housing, undermining cities' ability to match skills to jobs. Our analysis shows that between 2000 and 2010 population density dynamics within Mexican cities changed considerably. Most Mexican cities have experienced a significant drop in the number of people living in central areas, accompanied by increasing population densities in urban peripheries. Eighteen of Mexico's largest cities lost more than 20 percent of their central city population during the period. At the same time, economic activities and jobs remain in the city centers. Jobs consistently have a much steeper density gradient than population in Mexico. These trends are not limited to smaller or less dynamic cities: Hermosillo, Léon, Matamoros, Monterrey, Puebla, and Queretaro. Map ES.1 shows the variation in population densities in Monterrey with people concentrating on the outskirts of the city center, whereas the center has low population density (mostly in green). In contrast, map ES.2 shows higher job densities in the center of Monterrey (darker brown). Bringing both trends together, figure ES.1 shows the growing distance between jobs and housing.

The lack of mixed-use development and diversified employment subcenters has also affected the cities' ability to sort economic activities in space. The recent peri-urban development has been mostly single use and residential purpose. Creating employment subcenters can help cities to take advantage of economic clusters and agglomeration economies in strategic locations. Similarly, urban centers in Mexican cities remain underused and depopulated; and promoting revitalization and densification of the urban core, for instance by increasing the provision of affordable housing in inner cities, would help to bring people closer to their jobs. In the United States, cities developed subcenters through zoning and financial incentives, which Mexican cities could adapt.

Most urban economies in Mexico, especially in large cities, have stagnated into the nontradable, low value-added service sector, missing opportunities to reap

Map ES.1 Distribution of Population in Monterrey, 2010

Persons per hectare
- 0–33
- 34–79
- 80–128
- 129–360

Source: World Bank analysis based on data from the National Institute of Statistics and Geography (*Instituto Nacional de Estadística y Geografía*, INEGI).

Map ES.2 Distribution of Jobs in Monterrey, 2010

Jobs per hectare
- 0–2
- 3–6
- 7–14
- 15–370

Source: World Bank analysis based on data from the National Institute of Statistics and Geography (*Instituto Nacional de Estadística y Geografía*, INEGI).
Note: Job density is shown by Basic Geostatistical Area/Census Tract (*Área Geoestadística Básica*). These are the equivalent of census tracts in other countries and roughly correspond to neighborhoods containing an average of 1,900 residents and covering 40 hectares.

benefits from agglomeration economies. Although the service sector has been growing across Mexican cities, growth in this sector is more pronounced in large cities that were traditionally based on manufacturing. However, the rapid expansion of services in Mexican cities has failed to translate into high value-added activities, such as finance, insurance, technology, and telecommunications. For instance, the service sector generates over 50 percent of employment and

Figure ES.1 Population and Job Density by Distance to City Center, Monterrey

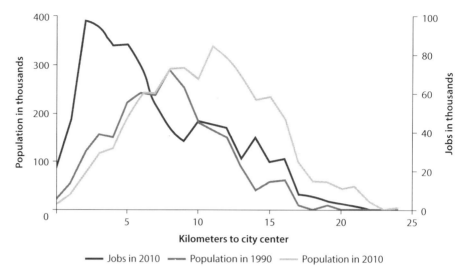

Source: World Bank diagram based on data from the National Institute of Statistics and Geography (*Instituto Nacional de Estadística y Geografía,* INEGI).
Note: There are no data available at the census tract level for 1990.

60 percent of GVA in Mexico City, four times the 15 percent seen in 1990. But nearly all that growth has pooled in the low value-added tier. Low value-added service activities expanded and now make up 54 percent of jobs in the service sector, and the share of high value-added activities has been declining since 2010.

The current model of urban expansion increased the cost of infrastructure and strains public services. The high costs of providing infrastructure for sprawling growth limit municipal resources, and are passed on to firms through fees and taxes. They also reduce the capacity of municipalities to support economic productivity outside the construction sector. Our analysis shows that municipalities with the lowest density had nearly 1.5 times as much municipal spending on public works and infrastructure per capita in 2010. Scenario planning available for different urban growth trajectories also shows that more compact urban development could save cities up to 70 percent of infrastructure and maintenance costs.

Economic potential and possible synergies of Mexican cities are left untapped because of a lack of coordination at the metropolitan and regional levels. Coordination among municipal administrations that form part of Mexican metropolises is still incipient, and there are few effective mechanisms for multi-jurisdictional and vertical coordination. Our case study contrasting the Monterrey (enforcing cycles of productivity growth and metropolitan coordination) and Oaxaca (stagnancy and isolation without coordination) metropolitan areas exemplifies how metropolitan governance can help to capitalize on contiguous municipalities and regional economics.

Moving toward More Inclusive and Livable Cities

As Mexican cities have been expanding, low-income households have been moving farther away from economic activities to new affordable housing developments in the urban periphery that lack adequate access to jobs, services, and urban amenities. The type of urban expansion in Mexican cities differs from the urban sprawl and suburbanization in the United States during the 1960s and 1970s. The U.S. suburbanization is often associated with middle-class households moving to suburbs for more space with better urban amenities. Although Mexico's middle class has also suburbanized, Mexico's housing development was mostly low-income housing. And it was not accompanied by infrastructure investment and coordination between housing financiers and municipalities.

Mexico's haphazard urban expansion has exacerbated spatial disparities in service and urban amenities and has limited the potential of cities to nurture inclusive development and improve livability for all urban residents. Cities in Mexico have reached almost universal coverage of basic services, yet problems in quality in the provision of service persist. More important, public service coverage can vary *within* cities as they sprawl without corresponding infrastructure, service networks, and urban amenities. The analysis in Guadalajara shows such trends: access to water, sewerage, and electricity remains low in the urban periphery, especially in the south where most of the recent urban expansion took place, whereas central areas are well served (see map ES3).

Similarly, the spatial growth in Mexican cities also brings negative environmental externalities, primarily resulting from increased congestion and commuting requirements. Limited access to public transportation has been the important bottleneck in recent peri-urban development, affecting time and money spent on transportation, particularly for low-income residents. The Guadalajara case study also shows that the recent housing development in the periphery is not covered by the public transportation system and that low-income people living in the urban periphery spend more of their income on transportation. In Mexico City, low-income households living in peri-urban areas can spend an additional four hours commuting per week. Increased burden on commuting increases greenhouse gas emissions and worsens air quality.

Policy Messages and Recommendations

Reframing the Policy Lens for Productive and Inclusive Urban Growth

Current housing policies can encourage dense and connected growth. Although housing policy reform in the 2000s provided more affordable housing, it also produced single-function, segregated residential developments in peri-urban areas. The government has recognized the problems associated with this model of housing production—particularly in the face of growing abandonment rates. And new policies to create more livable spaces are being introduced, such as differentiated up-front subsidies depending on the location. Supporting social

Map ES.3 Access to Infrastructure and Quality of Services in Guadalajara, 2000

Infrastructure index
- Very high
- High
- Low
- Very low
- No data

0 1 2   4 Miles

Source: World Bank analysis based on census data from the National Institute of Statistics and Geography (*Instituto Nacional de Estadística y Geografía*, INEGI).
Note: The Infrastructure Index for Guadalajara was generated using the INEGI census data. The index looks at the total number of houses per census tract that lack water infrastructure, drainage, or electricity and is then normalized by the total number of inhabited houses in the census tract. These values are then summed to create the final index values. The index values were calculated by using quartiles, which were defined as the following four categories: very low (0.138–2.00), low (0.021–0.137), high (0.006–0.020), and very high (0–0.005).

housing in planned and strategic locations within cities can help low-income households, offering them alternatives for affordable housing in the urban core.

But housing policies alone will not be enough; urban policies on planning, financing, and connecting should play a more prominent role in guiding spatial growth of Mexican cities. In Mexico, most policy response and instruments to influence urban spatial growth have been led by housing policies. Urban policies and instruments should promote smart urban growth and coordinate housing policies with broader urban development issues—particularly service plans, land use decisions, and infrastructure provisions—to reach a higher quality of life for all residents. Planning livable, productive, and sustainable cities is not merely about providing low-income housing or attaining high-density and compact development. Instead, cities should also facilitate a higher quality of life for their present and future residents—by providing good basic services to all residents regardless of location, income, or any other variable.

Current urban policy would benefit from broadening its focus on controlling urban expansion and considering multifaceted urban form in policy design. Urban growth should not be a cause for concern by itself, but rather it is the problems created by inefficient urban expansion that policy makers need to worry about. This Review shows that urban form is multidimensional and complex; hence, limiting the growth of cities across the board cannot be the main, nor the sole, point of action. Instead, it is critical to analyze the differences in urban form of different cities and understand the negative effects of urban expansion patterns. What is more important and relevant is to assess city-level density and spatial form, and to work on planning issues on a case-by-case approach and at a more granulated level. To this end, urban policy could benefit from shifting toward a more proactive spatial growth management that addresses effective planning and land use coordination with infrastructure to promote more productive and inclusive cities.

Policies that frame cities as the engines of economic growth can help pinpoint the bottlenecks in the urbanization process that slow economic growth and productivity at the city and regional level. Although cities are the center of production and growth for Mexico's economy, the current policy framework falls short of recognizing their economic role to promote growth and prosperity. A policy focus on the patterns of urban growth can better help design policies for cities to achieve their productive potential.

Planning for More Productive and Livable Mexican Cities

Incentivizing mixed land use zoning for peri-urban expansion and dilapidated urban cores is an immediate action that could ameliorate the negative aspects of new developments. Policies that encourage mixed land use can reduce home-to-work commuting trips and traffic-related environmental problems. If residential areas concentrate in the periphery of cities, a more effective approach to planning would be to decentralize jobs and amenities, and to create other urban centers that can also offer jobs, schools, commercial activities, and other amenities at shorter distances than the traditional center. Similarly, existing vacant and underused urban centers can be redeveloped into livable and affordable residential areas.

A metropolitan approach to policies, such as metro-level plans for subcenters, can also balance jobs and housing. This would require strong federal, state, and local efforts to identify appropriate locations for development, invest in the infrastructure for these developments, and create the financial incentives for homebuyers and developers to support more sustainable housing. And spatial development policies at the metropolitan level can effectively contain urban sprawl. There is a role for public policy in addressing market failures associated with the creation of alternate employment subcenters, given the limited incentives that exist for private firms to relocate away from the central business district, even after the benefits of agglomeration economies in this area are outweighed by negative externalities such as congestion and overcrowding.

Strengthening local capacities for urban planning can enable efficient and inclusive spatial growth. At both the state and municipal levels, low capacity and lack of resources have resulted in limited urban and land use planning functions to preparing plans for future urban growth as well as specific investment projects. A recent survey to assess urban development plans covering the 59 metropolitan areas encompassing 367 municipalities (World Bank and CMM 2016) demonstrated limited planning capacity available at the municipal level. For instance, about one-third of the surveyed municipalities does not have any spatial information as part of their Municipal Urban Development Plan, and a majority of the municipalities had the information in inadequate or obsolete formats. Of the plans surveyed, only about 13 percent had a metropolitan approach. Furthermore, about 38 percent did not specify a planning period, whereas 40 percent of the plans are valid until 2030 with no clear indication of review and update before the plan expires. Many municipalities in Mexican cities lack spatial planning capacity and do not develop a strategic vision for future growth—and plan accordingly—but instead focus on separate sectoral programs. The federal government can consider strengthening planning institutes to support capacity building of different localities. It can take the lead in providing land use guidelines and best practices, as well as creating benchmarks for performance and compliance with planning requirements among municipalities. In addition, the federal government can consider developing incentive programs that aim to better articulate long-term vision for city development, and better integrate land use planning, housing development, and transport investment.

Connecting Institutions and Coordination

Coordination is a cross-cutting policy priority for all institutions involved in urban and housing policies. Close coordination among housing, infrastructure, transport, and services is key to helping peri-urban developments bridge the service gap and reach a higher quality of life for all residents. Economic potentials and possible synergies of Mexican cities are left untapped because of a lack of coordination at the metropolitan and regional levels.

Strengthening metropolitan and regional coordination can unlock economies of scale for public investment and planning. Currently, there is no real legal provision for a metropolitan government structure. Metropolitan areas are managed by municipal governments that make up the metropolitan areas, and there is no clear regional framework for sharing responsibilities and resources. And vertical alignment and coordination between federal and local governments need common objectives and incentives for sustainable spatial development.

Improving vertical alignment of priorities and coordinating planning between federal and local governments can ensure more efficient and equitable urban growth. Current national urban and housing policies incentivize and direct local development, but efforts to coordinate with different agencies or local government have been limited. The task of coordinating agencies cannot be underestimated, but there are relatively few mechanisms to coordinate with municipal, metropolitan, or state visions for sustainable housing and urban land use. One important way to address the spatial structure of cities is to have municipal governments participate in housing programs, decisions, and building processes.

The federal government can provide incentives. The right incentives for state and municipal governments would align the national policy objectives, such as compact and sustainable urban development, with local land use decisions. For instance, the federal government could work with local governments to promote urban redensification by piloting financial incentives. It could also partner with planning institutions to strengthen local planning capacities and take a more active role coordinating different levels of government and agencies working on urban issues. One immediate example would be to improve coordination between the urban and housing policies promoted by the Ministry for Rural, Territorial, and Urban Development (*Secretaria de Desarrollo Agrario, Territorial y Urbano*, SEDATU) and the infrastructure and transport investment by the National Works and Public Services Bank (*Banco Nacional de Obras y Servicios Públicos*, BANOBRAS).

Financing for Well-Connected, Prosperous, and Livable Cities

Extending access to basic services in marginalized urban areas and lagging regions is a step to incorporate peri-urban settlements into the urban fabric and achieve the "last miles" of universal access and high-quality basic services. Current policy relies heavily on housing subsidies to promote dense urban areas. Although housing subsidies can contribute to more sustainable cities, other financing instruments are needed to get local governments, private housing developers, and the financial sector to work together. Land-based financing can pay for upgrading urban infrastructure with betterment levies, developer land sales, value capture through project-related land sales, development rights sales, developer exactions and impact fees, and land asset management.

Strategic redevelopment of inner cities in partnership with the private sector can provide affordable housing and regenerate downtown areas for economic activities. Redensifying and regenerating urban centers makes inner cities more attractive and livable. A few pilot projects for urban regeneration led by the federal government with local authorities are in a nascent stage. The government could set up a framework for inner-city regeneration and set incentives for local governments to revitalize inner cities and expand the pilot projects with private sector participation.

Supporting such financing with well-functioning cadastral systems for Mexican cities is another important action. Fluid land markets and systems to monitor and update movement help cities manage inner-city regeneration programs with the private sector. In particular, land-based financing supports infrastructure projects by tapping into the increments in land values from investment. Well-functioning cadastral systems are important for innovative financing to work. Cadastral systems in Mexico are generally fragmented and delegated to municipal levels without harmonized methods and standardized technology. There is much room for the federal government to invest in local capacities to manage cadastral systems.

Note

1. Approximately 4.5 million mortgages were provided by INFONAVIT between 2000 and 2012 whereas only half of that amount was delivered between 1972 and 2000. The housing deficit in Mexico has fallen 6 percentage points in the past decade.

Reference

World Bank and CMM (Centro Mario Molina). 2015. *Perfil Metropolitano: Escenarios de Crecimiento y Capacidad de Carga Urbana en 59 Zonas Metropolitanas*. Mexico City, Mexico: Centro Mario Molina para Estudios Estratégicossobre Energía y MedioAmbiente.

Abbreviations

AGEB	Basic Geostatistical Area/Census Tract (*Area Geoestadistica Básica*)
BRT	bus rapid transit
BANOBRAS	National Works and Public Services Bank (*Banco Nacional de Obras y Servicios Públicos*)
CI	centrality index
CLI	clustering index
CMM	Centro Mario Molina
CONAPO	National Population Council (*Consejo Nacional de Población*)
CONAVI	National Housing Commission (*Comisión Nacional de Vivienda*)
CONEVAL	National Council for the Evaluation of Social Development Policy (*Consejo Nacional de Evaluación de la Política de Desarrollo Social*)
CORETT	Landownership regularization commission (*Comisión para la Regularización de la Tenencia de la Tierra*)
FONHAPO	National Fund for Popular Housing (*Fideicomiso Fondo Nacional de Habitaciones Populares*)
FOVISSSTE	Housing Fund of the Social Security and Services Institute for State Workers (*Fondo de la Vivienda del Instituto de Seguridad y Servicios Sociales de los Trabajadores del Estado*)
GDP	gross domestic product
GMA	Guadalajara Metropolitan Area
GVA	gross value added
HDI	Human Development Index
IMCO	Mexican Institute for Competitiveness (*Instituto Mexicano para la Competitividad*)
IMECA	Air Quality Metropolitan Index (*Índice Metropolitano de la Calidad del Aire*)
IMPLAN	Municipal Planning Institute (*Instituto Municipal [o Metropolitano] de Planeación*)

INEGI	National Institute of Statistics and Geography (*Instituto Nacional de Estadística y Geografía*)
INFONAVIT	Federal Institute for Workers' Housing (*Instituto del Fondo Nacional de la Vivienda para los Trabajadores*)
LISA	Local Indicators of Spatial Association
LRT	light rail train
MCMA	Mexico City Metropolitan Area
OECD	Organisation of Economic Co-operation and Development
PI	proximity index
RUV	National Housing Registry (*Registro Unico de Vivienda*)
SEDATU	Ministry for Rural, Territorial, and Urban Development (*Secretaria de Desarrollo Agrario, Territorial y Urbano*)
SEDESOL	Secretariat of Social Development (*Secretariat de Desarrollo Social*)
SEMARNAT	Secretariat of Environment and Natural Resources (*Secretaria de Medio Ambiente y Recursos Naturales*)
SHF	Federal Mortgage Society (*Socieded Hipotecaria Federal*)
SUN	National Urban System (*Sistema Urbano Nacional*)
UA	urbanized areas
UN	United Nations

CHAPTER 1

Setting the Scene

High Levels of Urbanization in Mexico

Mexico is at an advanced stage of urbanization, with nearly 77 percent of its population living in urban areas in 2010. Like many other Latin American countries, Mexico experienced rapid urbanization during the mid-20th century and became a predominantly urban country around 1960, when average annual urbanization growth rates reached 5 percent (figure 1.1). Although the pace has slowed since then, the population of Mexican cities continues to grow at an average rate of about 1.6 percent[1] per year (UN 2014).

Mexico has a consolidated system of cities that is relatively balanced across urban agglomerations of all sizes. In 2010, over 72 percent of Mexicans lived in the country's 384 cities that each have more than 15,000 inhabitants.[2] The Mexico City Metropolitan Area is by far the largest urban agglomeration in the country and the largest in Latin America, concentrating a quarter of Mexico's urban population in 2010 (20.1 million residents). However, big cities with between 1 and 10 million inhabitants have been gaining in importance over the past decade and are now home to 26 percent of the country's urban population. Another 20 percent and 17 percent of urban residents live in medium and small cities, respectively. In contrast, the 289 small towns with fewer than 100,000 inhabitants host only 12 percent (map 1.1 and table 1.1).

In contrast to other countries at comparable stages of urbanization, large cities continue to grow quickly in Mexico. Large cities that had more than 1 million inhabitants in 2010 have experienced average annual population growth of 4.9 percent between 1990 and 2010. The population living in medium cities has also been growing at 2.6 percent on average per year. In contrast, Mexico City and small cities with fewer than 100,000 inhabitants in 2010 have been growing less rapidly and have decreased their share of overall urban population since 1990 (see map 1.1 and table 1.1).

Mexican cities are distributed across the country's entire territory but are more concentrated in the center region. Given the size of Mexico, its system of cities can be subdivided into five distinct regions following the definition of the Mexican Central Bank: border, north, center, south, and capital.[3]

Figure 1.1 Population Growth and Urbanization in Mexico since 1900

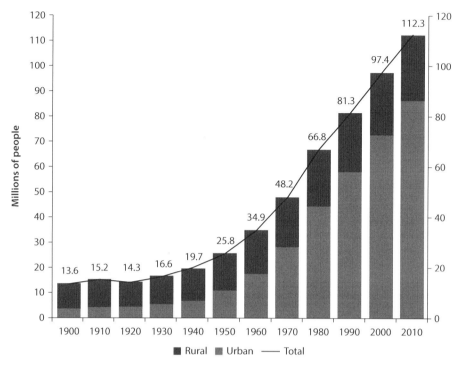

Source: Census data from the National Institute of Statistics and Geography (*Instituto Nacional de Estadística y Geografía*, INEGI).
Note: INEGI defines *urban population* as people living in a settlement with more than 2,500 inhabitants.

Map 1.1 Mexican Cities by Population Size

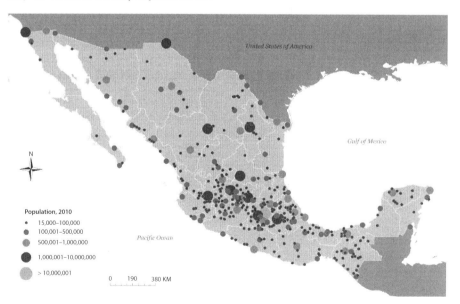

Source: World Bank analysis based on data from the Secretariat of Social Development (*Secretariat de Desarrollo Social,* SEDESOL).

Table 1.1 Distribution of Cities by Population Size in Mexico

City size	1990		2000		2010	
(pop. range in 2010)	No. of cities	Total pop.	No. of cities	Total pop.	No. of cities	Total pop.
Towns (>15k–100k)	228	7.5m (14%)	251	8.3m (12%)	289	9.4m (12%)
Small cities (>100k–500k)	51	12.2m (23%)	57	12.8m (19%)	62	13.9m (17%)
Medium cities (>500k–1m)	15	10m (19%)	19	12.7m (19%)	22	16.4m (20%)
Big cities (>1m–10m)	4	8.5m (16%)	8	15.7m (23%)	10	21.2m (26%)
Megacity (>10m)	1	15.6m (29%)	1	18.4m (27%)	1	20.1m (25%)
Total	299	53.8m	336	67.9m	384	81m

Source: World Bank analysis based on data from the Secretariat of Social Development (*Secretariat de Desarrollo Social,* SEDESOL).

Although there are important urban centers in each region and smaller cities are spread across the country, nearly all large cities with more than 1 million inhabitants cluster around Mexico City in the center region and close to the border with the United States. The central area of Mexico is generally more densely populated than the southern and northern parts of the country (map 1.2 and table 1.2).

Urbanization and Socioeconomic Achievements in Mexico

As in other countries, urbanization in Mexico has been associated with increased prosperity and improvements in quality of life. Urban areas lead in expanding coverage of basic and social services. Since the decentralization of the provision of public services started in 1983, water and sanitation coverage has become almost universal in most Mexican cities. In contrast, rural areas continue to face greater challenges in the provision of water and sanitation services. There are still 7.2 million rural residents without access to potable water service and even 13.2 million who do not have basic sanitation; these figures in urban areas have been reduced to 1.6 million and 3.8 million, respectively (Collado 2008). Cities also offer better access to other services and amenities, including health care and education. Moreover, Mexico's growing middle class and declining inequality in recent decades seem to be decidedly urban phenomena (Ferreira 2013).

Urbanization in Mexico has also gone hand in hand with economic growth. Given the sustained rate of urbanization in Mexico, global experiences suggest major benefits have accrued in productivity growth and equity (World Bank 2009). And, indeed, as cities were growing rapidly and industrialization promoted by the national government was ongoing, Mexico experienced strong economic growth—with real gross domestic product (GDP) growing on average by 6.5 percent per year between 1950 and 1981 (Kehoe and Meza 2011). GDP per capita increased tenfold in this period, from US$540 to over US$5,970 (Kehoe and Meza 2011). Since 1980, Mexico's GDP and GDP per capita have continued to grow steadily albeit at relatively low annual average growth rates of 2.4 percent and 0.7 percent, respectively.

Map 1.2 Categorization of Mexican Cities by Geographical Location

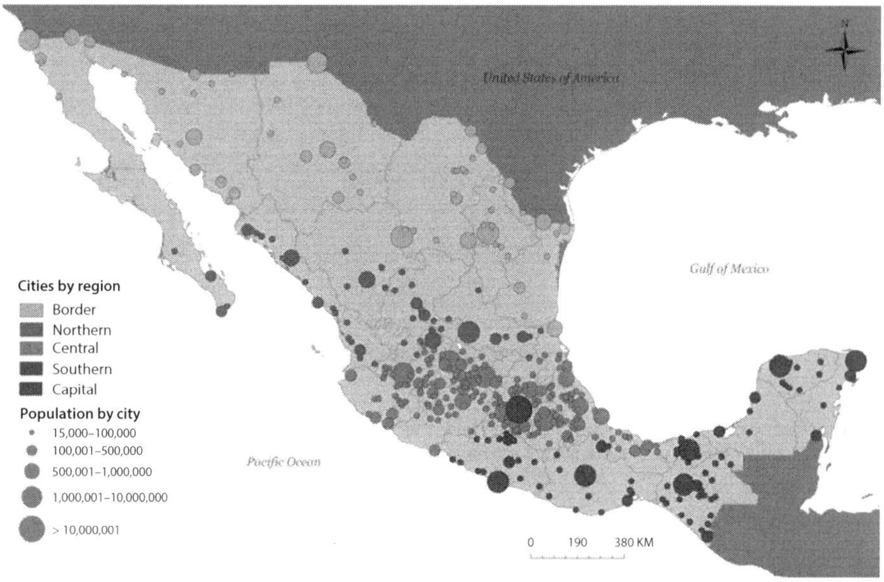

Source: World Bank analysis based on data from the Secretariat of Social Development (*Secretariat de Desarrollo Social,* SEDESOL).

Table 1.2 Geographic Distribution of Cities in Mexico

	1990		2000		2010	
Region	No. of cities (pop. >15k)	Total pop.	No. of cities (pop. >15k)	Total pop.	No. of cities (pop. >15k)	Total pop.
Capital	1	15.5m (29%)	1	18.4m (27%)	1	21.1m (26%)
Border	54	11.3m (21%)	57	14.7m (22%)	62	18.1m (22%)
North	40	3.9m (7%)	43	5m (7%)	52	6.4m (8%)
Center	144	18.4m (34%)	161	23.2m (34%)	179	28.1m (34%)
South	60	4.7m (9%)	74	6.6m (10%)	90	8.5m (10%)
Total	299	53.8m	336	67.9m	384	82.2m

Source: World Bank analysis based on data from the Secretariat of Social Development (*Secretariat de Desarrollo Social,* SEDESOL).

Remaining Challenge: Distant, Dispersed, and Disconnected Urban Spatial Growth

There have been important changes to the spatial form of Mexican cities over the past 30 years: most notably urban growth is characterized as distant, dispersed, and disconnected. Between 1980 and 2010, the built-up area of Mexican cities expanded on average by a factor of seven and the urbanized area of the eleven biggest metropolitan areas with more than 1 million inhabitants in 2010 has even grown by a factor of nine (SEDESOL 2012). This rapid spatial transformation of most Mexican cities presents important challenges for their potential to promote green and inclusive growth.

The housing sector has contributed disproportionately to the urban expansion through low-density, single-use large housing developments built on the outskirts of cities. Mexico initiated a radical transformation of its housing sector in 2000 (see box 1.1 for details on the evolution of housing policies in Mexico). Aided by macroeconomic stability and policy reform, the country successfully increased the supply of low-cost housing by about 1 million units each year between 2006 and 2011, totaling 7.1 million newly built individual houses during this period. These new units, most of which are single-story and single-family "horizontal" housing, have occupied about 60 percent of the land in new urban settlements. As housing developers sought to produce more housing units (for which substantial subsidies were available) while reducing the cost of land (for which no financing support was available), they acquired rural land plots distant from city centers. These plots were later transformed into urban land on a plot-by-plot basis, resulting in a patched urban pattern.

Box 1.1 Housing Policies in Mexico

Although public initiatives in housing go back at least a century in Mexico, the last 50 years have experienced an acceleration in governmental involvement in the sector. Since the mid-1950s, a series of entities began to provide units, often through direct construction. Many of these were for formal private and public sector employees, to fulfill the constitutional guarantees of housing for workers (Article 123 of the Mexican Constitution). When the mechanisms of provision shifted to finance and demand subsidies after the mid-1990s, the scale of public programs increased, and today nearly one in four Mexicans lives in a home financed by the Federal Institute for Workers' Housing (*Instituto del Fondo Nacional de la Vivienda para los Trabajadores*, INFONAVIT), the largest source of loans in Mexico and Latin America, with over 5 million mortgages on its books. INFONAVIT functions as a tripartite entity run by affiliated workers, companies, and the federal government.

The reform of housing policies and expansion of INFONAVIT in the early 2000s led to an important transformation of the housing production system in Mexico: more houses were built by private developers and purchased with a mortgage than through self-build construction. Receiving 5 percent of all formal workers' salaries, INFONAVIT provides several housing-related mortgage products, including mortgages to buy a new or existing home, to remodel, or to build a new one. Approximately 4.5 million mortgages were provided by INFONAVIT between 2000 and 2012—whereas only half of that amount was delivered between 1972 and 2000. Reflecting these efforts, the housing deficit in Mexico has fallen 6 percentage points in the past decade.

The combination of operational, structural, and financial improvements of INFONAVIT, the housing and mortgage markets, and stable macroeconomic conditions allowed the government and industry to reach out to larger and more economically diverse segments of the population to finance their homes. Production of new homes has increased dramatically, and financing options have been greatly expanded in previously underserved markets. At the

box continues next page

Box 1.1 Housing Policies in Mexico *(continued)*

same time, the share of workers unaffiliated with the social security system and therefore ineli-
gible to borrow from INFONAVIT (and the Housing Fund of the Social Security and Services
Institute for State Workers—*Fondo de la Vivienda del Instituto de Seguridad y Servicios Sociales
de los Trabajadores del Estado*, FOVISSSTE) fell from 64 percent in 2000 to 55 percent in 2010.

In order to increase its lending options to a wider range of workers, INFONAVIT concentrated federal housing subsidies on the low-income end and expanded co-financing for
higher income workers. Significant efforts have been made using federal subsidies to support
households that earn fewer than four minimum wages (that come from the National Housing
Commission, the National Fund for Popular Housing, or the Federal Mortgage Society).[a] In
2011, 63 percent of all INFONAVIT mortgages were issued to workers in this category.
Furthermore, in the past decade, housing policies and financers have also worked to provide
support to a wider range of housing needs, such as financing for self-help for very low income
households, funding to acquire lots with services, progressive housing, improvements to existing homes, and the acquisition of existing housing in the formal sector. One aspect of housing
finance that remains undeveloped is financing for rental housing.

Despite the advances made on the quantitative production of new houses for a wider
range of workers, there are still 9.04 million homes that are overcrowded or in need of repairs
and a demand of approximately 500,000 new units a year to meet population growth in the
next decade. A large share of new demand for housing comes from workers with modest
incomes, which incentivizes developers to build on cheaper land in the urban periphery.
Simultaneously, INFONAVIT and FOVISSSTE continue to seek ways to provide more loans to
lower income households, further encouraging developers to build homes on affordable, yet
peripheral, areas.

Sources: Ballantine 2014; Herber 2012.
a. The minimum salary in 2015 is reported as Mex$2,046.6.

Reform Agenda for Urban and Housing Policies

The current government has recognized the challenges associated with continu-
ous urban sprawl and the importance of density for sustainable urban development. The Peña Nieto administration, which took office in December 2012, aims
to promote sustainable urban and housing policies as part of the government's
broader efforts toward making Mexico more inclusive. Specifically, under the
second pillar of the 2013–2018 National Development Plan (*Plan Nacional de
Desarrollo*, PND) the government aims to (i) improve institutional coordination
within the housing and urban sectors, (ii) gradually transition toward a more
sustainable urban spatial pattern, (iii) responsibly reduce the housing deficit, and
(iv) promote diverse and affordable housing solutions for the population.

The National Urban and Housing Programs 2013–2018, released in July 2013
(SEDATU 2013), articulate the consolidation of existing urban areas and limiting
spatial expansion of cities as key priorities of the new policy. Other priorities of the
sectoral programs include the provision of sustainable and dignified housing
through the diversification of financing and subsidy options as well as housing

solutions, promotion of sustainable urban transport, improving land management, and introducing better territorial planning systems at the local and regional level. The government is also in the process of further refining existing federal housing programs, including the main housing subsidy program "This Is Your House" (*Esta es Tu Casa*), to better align with the new policy priorities. Specifically, it started to implement differentiated subsidies and location-specific housing credits to discourage peri-urban expansion and encourage the redensification of inner cities.

The Ministry of Agrarian, Territorial, and Urban Development (*Secretaria de Desarrollo Agrario, Territorial y Urbano*, SEDATU)[4] calls for the concentration and redensification of the housing stock in the inner cities by introducing location-specific housing credits and subsidies in order to discourage peri-urban expansion. Efforts have been put into generating a System of Geostatistical Information on Urban Development, Land, and Housing that established urban contention perimeters (*perímetros de contención urbana*) for each city that are being applied to determine housing subsidies to limit the expansion of urban areas. Development and construction outside those limits would be controlled (*desarrollos certificados*). Furthermore, through the new model, the Government of Mexico aims to create urban land reserves—considered "developable"—in the outskirts of urban and metropolitan areas, and will equip them with infrastructure and basic services, as necessary for future growth.

The creation of a unified National Housing Registry (*Registro Unico de Vivienda*, RUV) was an important step for implementing the recent policy reform, in particular regarding the location of housing. The RUV, established by law in 2004, became operational in 2009. Since then, new housing being developed in Mexico is registered with RUV, which collects relevant data on national housing supply, including property value, progress of construction, location, housing characteristics, and quality of housing. RUV has become an important source of information to improve decision making of both public and private actors involved in the provision of housing. It also serves as a screening mechanism to calculate the location-based point and eligibility of prospective housing developments for the federal housing subsidy program.

The government has also made significant efforts to put in place measurement systems and to broaden information about urban dynamics. An ambitious national initiative, the National Urban System (*Sistema Urbana Nacional*, SUN), proposes to create a unified platform to support decision making for urban and housing policies. The SUN, launched by Mexican federal agencies in 2012, marks a significant effort to broaden information and understanding about urban dynamics and has been recognized as innovative among Latin American urban initiatives. See box 1.2 for details of the classification of city types on which the SUN is based.

Objectives and Scope of the *Mexico Urbanization Review*

In light of the government's new policy priorities, this Urbanization Review sets out to analyze recent spatial patterns of Mexican cities, their causes, and their impact and to provide an analytical basis to understand how well-managed

Box 1.2 The National Urban System and Classification of City Types

To make sense of the quantities and types of cities that are shaping up in Mexico, the National Population Council (Consejo Nacional de Población, CONAPO) and the Secretariat of Social Development (*Secretariat de Desarrollo Social*, SEDESOL) put together the National Urban System (*Sistema Urbana Nacional*, SUN) on the basis of data from the Population and Housing Census (2010). The objective was to create a system to support strategic planning and decision making in urban areas and to provide all sectors (state governments, municipalities, academia, private sector, and general users) with integrated metropolitan and urban information on demographic and socioeconomic variables. The system comprises 384 cities with over 15,000 inhabitants each, out of which 59 are metropolitan areas, 78 conurbations (suburban centers), and 247 urban centers. About 81.2 million people or 72.3 percent of the country's population live in these 384 cities.

Mexican federal government agencies (CONAPO, SEDESOL, and the National Institute of Statistics and Geography [*Instituto Nacional de Estadistica y Geografia*, INEGI]) define a spatial clustering of 2,500 or more people as an urban area but consider those places with more than 15,000 people as cities.

The SUN defines three types of cities, classified on the basis of geographical delimitations used in the census (urban localities, among others) and administrative boundaries (SEDESOL and CONAPO 2012):

1. *Metropolitan areas* include three kinds of urban areas: (i) a group of municipalities that share a central city and are highly integrated, (ii) urban centers within one municipality that have a population of greater than 1 million, and (iii) urban centers on the U.S.–Mexico border with more than 250,000 residents.
2. *Urban conurbations* are urban areas that extend across more than one locality[a] and have more than 15,000 residents.
3. *Urban centers* are cities that have more than 15,000 residents and that do not extend beyond the boundaries of their locality.

Metropolitan areas are obtained from a delimitation exercise conducted by SEDESOL and CONAPO (2012). Conurbations are identified by looking at the layer of urban polygons of the geostatistical framework, version 5.0 of INEGI. Geostatistical urban localities with more than 15,000 inhabitants, which were not metropolitan or suburban areas, were classified as urban centers.

Source: SEDESOL and CONAPO 2012.
a. *Localities* are geostatistical areas defined by INEGI for the census named by law or by local tradition. Their technical definition is the area around one or more housing units, with groupings of dwellings with a population of over 2,500 deemed an urban locality.

urban growth can further contribute to unlocking the gains from urbanization. The report analyzes the spatial development patterns of Mexican cities since 1990 and reviews how policy actions have resulted in uncoordinated urban expansion. It reviews the performance and challenges of systems of cities for promoting productive, livable, and inclusive development and how well-managed urban spatial growth can accelerate the transition toward a high-income economy. Based on the analysis, it provides policy recommendations for urban growth that can help cities in Mexico improve their productivity and equity (box 1.3).

The analysis focuses on how city growth has supported or limited cities' potentials to increase efficiency/productivity and livability/inclusiveness. Overall, urbanization and growing cities offer opportunities to improve Mexicans' economic and social development. However, poorly planned, inefficient peri-urban growth can dampen cities' potential to boost productivity and shared prosperity (see box 1.4 for definition of peri-urban). When housing is located in remote areas without access to transportation and other urban services, residents lose access to employment opportunities and their individual productivity is likely to decrease as a result of increasing time spent commuting to work. The situation

---

Box 1.3 What Is an Urbanization Review?

The World Bank's Urbanization Reviews (URs) form a global analytical program that studies the urbanization process of countries, focusing on the main urban challenges and policy implications. The UR follows a framework that aims to help policy makers and city leaders make informed decisions to support sustainable urban development in their countries. It provides diagnostic tools that inform policy and investment priorities to improve the living conditions of urban populations, create jobs, increase productivity, and develop inclusive urban spaces, with equal access to basic services. Moreover, URs help leaders develop a comprehensive set of guidelines to make cities more productive, inclusive, and sustainable, ultimately taking better advantage of urbanization processes to reduce poverty and promote shared prosperity.

The diagnostic approach used in this program looks at three main dimensions of urban development, and uses them as the base for putting together a set of guidelines:

1. *Planning* is about charting a course for cities by setting the terms of urbanization, especially policies for using urban land and expanding basic infrastructure and public services.
2. *Connecting* looks at how to make a city's markets (labor, goods, and services) accessible to other cities and to other neighborhoods in the city, as well as to outside export markets.
3. *Financing* finds sources for large capital outlays needed to provide infrastructure and services as cities grow and urbanization picks up speed.

The World Bank, in collaboration with city leaders and national policy makers, has completed a series of diagnostic analyses under the UR program in various countries, including Colombia, India, Indonesia, Vietnam, and Uganda. They all seek to create knowledge on urbanization challenges and show how policy and investment choices can affect the pace, magnitude, and impact of urbanization and city development. *Mexico Urbanization Review: Managing Spatial Growth for Productive and Livable Cities in Mexico* is part of this series.

The UR in Mexico focuses mainly on analyzing Mexico's urban growth and its effect on economic performance and livability, rather than on addressing a wide set of issues included in URs in other countries. An extensive body of research and literature on urban development issues already existed for Mexico because of its advanced stage of urbanization.

Box 1.4 Locating "Peri-Urban" Areas

"Peri-urban" or "peripheral" areas have attracted much of Mexico's urban growth during the past two decades and are discussed frequently in this report. Although these areas are easily recognizable by practitioners in Mexico, no precise formal definition is in common use. Nonetheless, in general, peri-urban areas are often classified by both (i) recent change in land use away from rural characteristics such as agriculture and (ii) deficits in the urban characteristics, such as low accessibility and poor infrastructure (Allen 2003). Sánchez (2009) adds inadequate property titling and registration and social changes as common aspects of peri-urban development in Mexico. Across this review, the terms will be used interchangeably for areas that meet these two broad criteria, and specific sections will use more precise subsets and definitions for analysis. Similar terms, such as exurban, *rurbano*, semi-urban, suburban, and urban fringe, often overlap in meaning but will be avoided for purposes of clarity.

also affects the productivity of firms that can no longer take advantage of the city's entire labor market and may lose out on positive externalities associated with economic density. Similarly, local governments are not able to optimize the costs of building and maintaining required infrastructure and service provision. As commuting times and reliance on private cars increase, traffic congestion and associated air pollution also increase—lowering environmental sustainability and citizens' quality of life.

In order to analyze the spatial patterns of Mexican cities and the effects of urban form on economic performance and inclusiveness, this study constructed five metrics to measure spatial structure of cities. In addition to commonly used densities of population and economic activity, urban spatial structure can also be understood by measuring the relative concentration of these activities in the center versus the periphery (centrality), and the fragmentation or compactness of the city over its land area. This report uses five metrics to measure the three primary dimensions of urban spatial structure. The most basic measure is (i) *density*, which is the number of people or jobs per hectare. Centrality is measured in two ways: as (ii) a *density gradient* that reflects the city's centrality by measuring the rate at which density declines at greater distances from the city center; and with (iii) a *centrality index* proposed by Galster et al. (2001) that measures the average distance of the population from the city center relative to the size of the city. Similarly, two measures are applied to capture different aspects of urban fragmentation or compactness: (iv) a *proximity index* developed by Angel et al. (2010) that measures the extent to which a city has a circular shape, which is the most economical of urban forms, without considering the intensity of land use in different areas of the city; and (v) a *clustering index* that measures the unequal concentration of people and jobs in certain areas across the larger urban space.[5] Details on the methodology of constructing the five spatial indexes are presented in appendix B.

The spatial metrics show heterogeneity of urban form depending on the geography, location, and size of cities. Generally, smaller cities have markedly different urban forms from medium-size and large cities (table 1.3). They have lower densities and steeper density gradients but slightly less centrality and more clustering. This difference is expected; as cities grow, the difference in overall value of land, and especially of land in the central city, increases. This affects the intensity of land use and thus urban form. The analysis also showed that northern cities are the most compact by a wide margin, whereas border cities have the lowest density and are the least centralized and less compact (table 1.4). On average, central and southern cities are similar to one another and fall between border and northern cities in terms of sprawl characteristics.[6] The analysis also suggests that more granulated understanding of driving forces of current urban growth is needed to come up with adequate policy measures.

More important, the metrics show that urban spatial form is multifaceted and multidimensional. The multifaceted nature of urban spatial structure is reflected by the fact that the five spatial measures are not consistently correlated with one another across the 100 largest cities in Mexico in 2010 (table 1.5). Out of the five spatial indexes, some measures are correlated; for example, density gradients are strongly related to the proximity index, which measures circularity). Clustering and centrality are also strongly associated. There is a notable lack of correlation between overall population density of cities and all measures other than centrality. The lack of a strong correlation between many of these measures suggests that judging a city's expansion by one indicator alone is inadequate.

Table 1.3 Average Measures of Urban Spatial Structure by City Size, 2010

Index/city size	Median	Mean
Density gradient (DG)		
Large cities	0.05	0.06
Medium cities	0.07	0.07
Small cities	0.09	0.15
Centrality Index (CI)		
Large cities	0.58	0.72
Medium cities	0.84	0.84
Small cities	0.78	0.83
Proximity Index (PI)		
Large cities	0.72	0.64
Medium cities	0.57	0.58
Small cities	0.61	0.60
Clustering Index (CLI)		
Large cities	0.31	0.32
Medium cities	0.35	0.33
Small cities	0.36	0.37

Note: Large cities have 1 to 10 million inhabitants, medium-size cities 500,000 to 1 million, and small cities 100,000 to 500,000 (according to SEDESOL data).

Table 1.4   Average Measures of Urban Spatial Structure by Region, 2010

	Region			
Variable	Border	North	Center	South
Density gradient	−0.30	0.35	0.08	−0.15
Centrality index	−0.23	0.12	0.07	−0.04
Proximity index	−0.21	0.00	−0.08	0.29
Clustering index	−0.17	0.38	0.04	−0.18
Number of cities	62	52	180	90
Number of large- or medium-size cities	25	12	38	16

Note: Large cities have over 500,000 inhabitants, and medium-size cities have between 100,000 and 500,000.

Table 1.5   Correlations between Measures of Urban Spatial Structure, 2010

Variable	Population	Density	Gradient	Centrality	Proximity
Population (log)	1.00	—	—	—	—
Population density	0.33*	1.00	—	—	—
Density gradient	−0.44*	0.03	1.00	—	—
Centrality	−0.03	0.51*	0.32*	1.00	—
Proximity	−0.21*	0.13	0.72*	0.20*	1.00
Clustering	−0.36*	0.07	0.34*	0.59*	0.16

Note: Spearman correlation coefficients are reported; * indicates significant at the 0.05 level. — = not available.

Similarly, overall population and employment densities do not give a good sense of the internal distribution of and relationship between these densities.

The *Mexico Urbanization Review* is structured in five chapters. After this overview of Mexico's urbanization and current urban policy context, chapter 2 illustrates the economic performance and development of Mexican cities, as well as their contributions to reducing poverty and promoting shared prosperity. Chapter 3 delves into the analysis of the implications of prevailing spatial development trends of Mexican cities for their productive potential. In the same way, chapter 4 analyzes how recent spatial expansion trends affect the potential of Mexican cities to enhance inclusiveness and livability. The last chapter provides policy recommendations that can help the government support cities to enhance their productivity and improve their livability through efficient spatial development.

Notes

1. Most of this continued urban growth actually stems from natural population growth, which is currently 1.2 percent. Only about 0.4 percent actually comes from rural–urban migration, which means that the rate of urbanization remains nearly the same.
2. Although INEGI classifies settlements with more than 2,500 inhabitants as urban, the National Urban System includes only those settlements with more than 15,000 inhabitants.

3. Following the economic regions defined by the Mexico Central Bank, Mexico is divided into five regions: (i) the border region includes the states of Baja California, Coahuila, Chihuahua, Nuevo Léon, Sonora, and Tamaulipas; (ii) the north includes Aguascalientes, Baja California Sur, Durango, Nayarit, San Luis Potosi, Sinaloa, and Zacatecas; (iii) the center includes Colima, Guanajuato, Hidalgo, Jalisco, Mexico, Michoacán, Morelos, Puebla, Querétaro, Tlaxcala, and Veracruz; (iv) the south includes Campeche, Chiapas, Guerrero, Oaxaca, Quintana Roo, Tabasco, and Yucatán and (v) the Metropolitan Area of Mexico City includes the Federal District and 60 other surrounding municipalities.

4. SEDATU was created in early 2013 to revert the institutional fragmentation that had prevailed within the urban and housing institutional setup in Mexico. SEDATU is responsible for the preparation of urban and housing policies as well as the coordination and supervision of their implementation.

5. We calculate this index in a similar way to that of a location quotient, inspired in this respect by the work on urban centrality by Pereira et al. (2013).

6. There are several likely reasons for the sprawling nature of border cities: they are generally younger cities, thus city centers have less historical pull; they have a larger share of manufacturing employment; they have larger shares of new housing development under INFONAVIT; and their border location often means that much of their commercial activity occurs in the United States (Alegria 2000).

References

Alegria, T. 2000. "Juntos pero no revueltos: Ciudades en la frontera México-Estados Unidos." *Revista Mexicana de Sociología* 62 (2): 89–107.

Allen, A. 2003. "Environmental Planning and Management of the Peri-Urban Interface: Perspectives on an Emerging Field." *Environment and Urbanization* 15 (1): 135–48.

Angel, S., J. Parent, D. L. Civco, and A. M. Blei. 2010. *Atlas of Urban Expansion.* Cambridge, MA: Lincoln Institute of Land Policy.

Ballantine, Jonathan. 2014. "Access to Affordable Housing in Latin America: Lessons from Argentina, Brazil and Mexico." *Cities Today*, October 10. http://cities-today.com /access-to-affordable-housing-in-latin-america-lessons-from-argentina-brazil-and -mexico/.

Collado, J. 2008. "Entorno de la provisión de los servicios públicos de agua potable en México." In *El agua potable en México*, edited by R. Olivares, Mexico City, Mexico: Asociación Nacional de Empresas de Agua y Saneamiento, A.C.

Ferreira, F. H. 2013. *Economic Mobility and the Rise of the Latin American Middle Class.* Washington, DC: World Bank.

Galster, G., R. Hanson, M. R. Ratcliffe, H. Wolman, S. Coleman, and J. Freihage. 2001. "Wrestling Sprawl to the Ground: Defining and Measuring an Elusive Concept." *Housing Policy Debate* 12 (4): 681–717.

Herber, C. E. 2012. *The State of Mexico's Housing—Recent Progress and Continued Challenges.* Cambridge, MA: Joint Center for Housing Studies Harvard University.

Kehoe, T. J., and F. Meza. 2011. "Catch- Up Growth Followed by Stagnation: Mexico, 1950–2010." *Latin America Journal of Economics* 48 (2): 227–68.

Perreira, R. H. M., V. Nadalin, L. Monasterio, and P. H. M. Albuquerque. 2013. "Urban Centrality." *Geographical Analysis* 45 (1): 77–89.

Sánchez, H. 2009. "Periurbanización y espacios rurales en la periferia de las ciudades." *Revista Estudios Agrarios - Procuraduría Agraria* 41: 93–123.

SEDATU (*Secretaria de Desarrollo Agrario, Territorial y Urbano*). 2013. *Programas Nacionales de Desarrollo Urbano y de Vivienda 2013–2018.* Mexico City, Mexico: SEDATU. http://www.economia.unam.mx/cedrus/descargas/PNDUyV_PNDUV_Corregido.pdf.

SEDESOL (*Secretariat de Desarrollo Social*). 2012. *La expansión de las ciudades 1980–2010.* Mexico City, Mexico: SEDESOL.

SEDESOL and CONAPO (*Consejo Nacional de Población*). 2012. *Sistema Urbano Nacional.* Mexico City, Mexico: SEDESOL.

UN (United Nations). 2014. *UN World Urbanization Prospects: The 2014 Revision.* New York: United Nations.

World Bank. 2009. *World Development Report 2009: Reshaping Economic Geography.* Washington, DC: World Bank.

CHAPTER 2

Understanding Economic Performance and Progress toward Shared Prosperity

Introduction

Cities are engines of economic growth and shared prosperity. Internationally, evidence from cities suggests that urbanization and density can spark innovation and productivity gains (World Bank 2009). Economic innovation and productivity in firms often grow most easily in connected and dense urban environments, where labor, knowledge, and new ideas are just a few minutes away (Ciccone and Hall 1993; Glaeser et al. 1992; Rosenthal and Strange 2004). Further, new sectors most likely to tap into growing global markets often incubate and grow best in cities (Storper and Venables 2004). In addition to fostering virtuous growth cycles by connecting people, jobs, and markets, well-functioning cities also provide quality services and urban amenities to all their residents and allow all segments of the population to benefit from increased prosperity.

This chapter examines the economic performance of Mexican cities in recent decades; it also looks at trends in shared prosperity and poverty reduction in urban areas in Mexico. It will first examine the contribution of cities to Mexico's overall economic production and their productivity, looking at trends by both city size group and regions. Then, it will explore how the economic structure of Mexican cities has evolved in recent decades. It will also discuss recent trends in poverty reduction and inequality in Mexican cities. Last, it will argue that recent urban spatial growth patterns and their repercussions have made it more difficult for Mexican cities to maximize the benefits from agglomeration.

Overview of Economic Performance of Mexican Cities

Mexico has a concentrated economic footprint that is dominated by the largest metropolitan regions. Mexico's gross domestic product (GDP) and GDP per capita have been steadily growing since 1980, albeit at low annual average growth rates of 3 percent and 1 percent, respectively (World Bank 2015). Cities continue to spur the majority of this growth. Today, 87 percent of Mexico's gross value added (GVA)[1] is produced in cities with population of more than 100,000. As seen in figure 2.1a and 2.1b, the Mexico City Metropolitan Area (MCMA) alone contributed a quarter of national GVA in 2010, although it covers less than 0.3 percent of the national territory. Large cities with a population of over

Figure 2.1 Contribution to Economic Production (Gross Value Added) by City Size

a. Contribution to national GVA by city size, 1990 and 2010

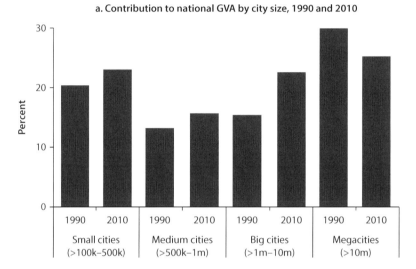

b. Contribution to overall GVA produced in cities with more than 100,000 inhabitants, 2009

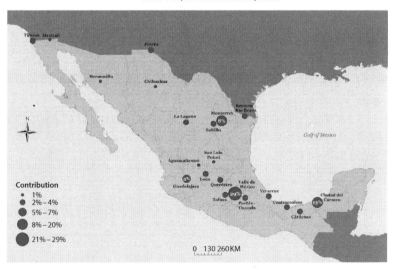

Source: World Bank analysis based on economic census data from the National Institute of Statistics and Geography (*Instituto Nacional de Estadística y Geografía,* INEGI).
Note: The bar graph shows each city size group's contribution to national GVA (including production in both urban and rural areas), whereas the map shows the contribution of selected cities to the overall GVA produced in cities with more than 100,000 inhabitants. GVA = gross value added.

1 million people contributed another 23 percent. Similarly, medium and small cities accounted for 16 and 23 percent of GVA in 2010, respectively (figure 2.1a).

Larger cities also tend to have greater labor productivity than smaller cities, with the notable exception of Mexico City. An initial analysis of municipalities calculated using panel data of 14,262 observations related to 2,377 municipalities over six years (1985, 1988, 1993, 1998, 2003, and 2008) suggests that there is a positive correlation between population size and labor productivity: for every additional 1,000 residents in a square kilometer, there is more than a quarter-percent increase in labor productivity GVA/l. Figure 2.2 also illustrates how labor productivity tends to increase with growing population, with the exception of Mexico City.

Cities in the central and border regions are leading in terms of economic production, whereas southern cities are lagging behind. Following Mexico City, cities in the central and border regions generate the largest shares of economic production (excluding mining sector). In 2010, cities in the central and border regions contributed over a quarter each to overall GVA produced in cities. In contrast, cities in the south and in the north each produced only about 5 percent of overall GVA from the manufacturing, services, and commerce sectors (see figure 2.3). Figure 2.3 also shows a clear north-south divide in terms of labor productivity. Whereas cities with the highest levels of productivity are mainly in the border

Figure 2.2 Correlation between City Size and Productivity in Mexico

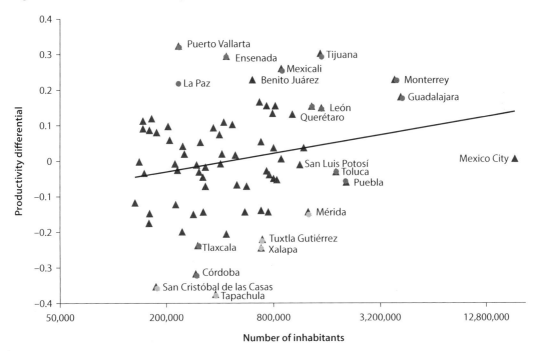

Source: Ahrend et al. 2014.
Note: Ahrend et al. 2014 defined *city productivity* as a wage premium associated with each city once the characteristics of the city workforce are taken into account. Cities were defined at the level of functional urban areas rather than on administrative boundaries. Southern cities are marked in green northern and central cities in orange.

Mexico Urbanization Review • http://dx.doi.org/10.1596/978-1-4648-0916-3

Figure 2.3 Contribution to Overall GVA Produced in Cities with More Than 100,000 Inhabitants by Region, 1990 and 2010

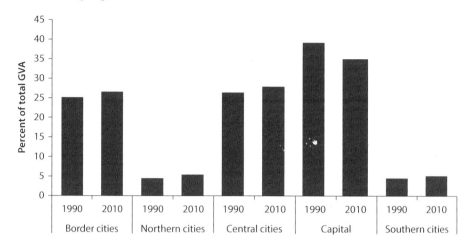

Source: World Bank analysis based on economic census data from the National Institute of Statistics and Geography (*Instituto Nacional de Estadística y Geografía*, INEGI).
Note: GVA = gross value added.

and central regions (for example, La Paz, Tijuana, and Monterrey), southern cities (for example, San Cristóbal de las Casas, Xalapa, and Mérida) and Mexico City are negative outliers in terms of productivity.

The existing urban policy framework could further benefit from recognizing the role of cities to promote economic growth and prosperity. Concentration of economic activity and population is not unique to Mexico. Half the world's production occurs on 1.5 percent of its land. In Japan, Tokyo has 4 percent of the country's land area but generates 40 percent of its output. In France, Paris has only 2 percent of the land but accounts for 30 percent of the country's output. Understanding the dynamics of economic structure, specialization, and productivity in urban areas that are part of regional and national systems of cities can enable informed policies that help unlock the potential of cities to fuel more economic growth. Considering existing differences in productive characteristics and urban growth patterns of cities in Mexico's five different economic regions (as defined by the Mexican Central Bank), the national policy could, for instance, be improved by articulating differentiated regional policy for economic development and specialization (see box 2.1 for a characterization of Mexico's economic regions).

Evolving Economic Structure of Mexican Cities

Research has shown that economic roles of cities are often determined by city size. The distribution of large, medium, and small cities is typically dictated by the distribution of economic activities. According to the trajectory suggested by urban economics literature, Mexico City and large cities would be expected to be nurseries for innovative activities and niche products, focusing on high value

Box 2.1 Economic Activity and Regional Dynamics: One Input for a Differentiated Policy Lens

Southern region: reliant on tourism, and susceptible to external shocks. Although most of the metropolitan areas have diversified in the manufacturing, commerce, and service sectors, the primary economic activity in the region continues to be oil, representing an average share of 84 percent of the country's economic production. Urban tourism resources are abundant, but the sector has been slow to grow over the last two decades.

Central region: diversifying, with leadership from high value-added manufacturing. The region has rapidly diversified into services and commerce. Although Guadalajara has dominated the service sector over the last twenty years, other cities such as Puebla-Tlaxcala, Morelia, and León also have taken a larger share of the service sector in the region. The main economic activity in the region is manufacturing, with an average share of 44 percent in 2009 relative to the rest of the country, followed by the commercial sector with 37 percent, services with 16 percent, and mining with 9 percent. The manufacturing sector is dominated by Guadalajara with a decreasing share over time of 22 percent in 1994, 21 percent in 1999, 17 percent in 2004, and 16 percent in 2009. While the metropolitan areas (MAs) of Queretaro, Pachuca, and Morelia were economic growth poles during the 1980s, they are now overshadowed by the growth shown mainly by Guadalajara, and also by Toluca, Puebla-Tlaxcala, Morelia, and León.

Northern region: commerce, but less access to manufacturing. Although a diverse group of strong cities specialize in separate sectors, overall the north continues to be dominated by clusters of commerce because of the heavy trade it has with the MAs of the border region and Mexico City. Eleven percent of the country's commerce comes from this region, followed by manufacturing (7 percent of the country's total) and services (5 percent). Culiacan's MA has dominated the commerce sector during the last 20 years, followed by San Luis Potosi's MA whereas San Luis Potosi's MA and Aguascalientes have traditionally specialized in the manufacturing sector. The services sector is dominated by La Paz's MA, followed by San Luis Potosi's. San Luis Potosi has shown the highest diversification across the different sectors, acting as the top-performing city in the north region.

Border region: strong manufacturing, and an economic base that spreads to other sectors. The region is still dominated by manufacturing, with an average participation of 32 percent relative to the country, followed by commerce with 24 percent, services with 19 percent, and mining with 9 percent. Of the 14 MAs localized in the border area, the top-performing MA is Monterrey, which has dominated the manufacturing sector but has also diversified, over time, to other sectors such as commerce and services. Monterrey dominates the services sector because of its financial subsector, where it is one of the national leaders. Other MAs that have followed in Monterrey's steps are Ciudad Juarez and Tijuana with strong economic and labor activity.

Capital (Valle de Mexico) Metropolitan Area: not leveraging urban agglomeration and with service-sector growth that continues to be low value added. The capital has the biggest participation in the GVA of the country for the services and commercial sectors, with participation of 56 percent and 19 percent, respectively, in 2009.[a]

Southern region: reliant on tourism, and susceptible to external shocks. Although most of the metropolitan areas have diversified in the manufacturing, commerce, and service sectors,

box continues next page

Box 2.1 Economic Activity and Regional Dynamics: One Input for a Differentiated Policy Lens
(continued)

the primary economic activity in the region continues to be oil, representing an average share of 84 percent of the country's economic production. Urban tourism resources are abundant, but the sector has been slow to grow over the last two decades.

Central region: diversifying, with leadership from high value added manufacturing. The region has rapidly diversified into services and commerce. Although Guadalajara has dominated the service sector over the last twenty years, other cities such as Puebla-Tlaxcala, Morelia, and León also have taken a larger share of the service sector in the region. The main economic activity in the region is manufacturing, with an average share of 44 percent in 2009 relative to the rest of the country, followed by the commercial sector with 37 percent, services with 16 percent, and mining with 9 percent. The manufacturing sector is dominated by Guadalajara with a decreasing share over time of 22 percent in 1994, 21 percent in 1999, 17 percent in 2004, and 16 percent in 2009. While the metropolitan areas (MAs) of Queretaro, Pachuca, and Morelia were economic growth poles during the 1980s, they are now overshadowed by the growth shown mainly by Guadalajara, and also by Toluca, Puebla-Tlaxcala, Morelia, and León.

Northern region: commerce, but less access to manufacturing. Although a diverse group of strong cities specialize in separate sectors, overall the north continues to be dominated by clusters of commerce because of the heavy trade it has with the MAs of the border region and Mexico City. Eleven percent of the country's commerce comes from this region, followed by manufacturing (7 percent of the country's total) and services (5 percent). Culiacan's MA has dominated the commerce sector during the last 20 years, followed by San Luis Potosi's MA whereas San Luis Potosi's MA and Aguascalientes have traditionally specialized in the manufacturing sector. The services sector is dominated by La Paz's MA, followed by San Luis Potosi's. San Luis Potosi has shown the highest diversification across the different sectors, acting as the top-performing city in the north region.

Border region: strong manufacturing, and an economic base that spreads to other sectors. The region is still dominated by manufacturing, with an average participation of 32 percent relative to the country, followed by commerce with 24 percent, services with 19 percent, and mining with 9 percent. Of the 14 MAs localized in the border area, the top-performing MA is Monterrey, which has dominated the manufacturing sector but has also diversified, over time, to other sectors such as commerce and services. Monterrey dominates the services sector because of its financial subsector, where it is one of the national leaders. Other MAs that have followed in Monterrey's steps are Ciudad Juarez and Tijuana with strong economic and labor activity.

Capital (Valle de Mexico) Metropolitan Area: not leveraging urban agglomeration and with service-sector growth that continues to be low value added. The capital has the biggest participation in the GVA of the country for the services and commercial sectors, with participation of 56 percent and 19 percent, respectively, in 2009.[a]

a. This data was taken from the 1989, 1994, 1999, 2004, and 2009 economic censuses generated by the National Institute of Statistics and Geography (*Instituto Nacional de Estadística y Geografía*, INEGI).

added service industry (for example, finance, R&D), whereas medium and smaller cities specialize in manufacturing and industries based on their natural comparative advantage of relatively low-cost land and labor.

Cities in Mexico are becoming more service-based; in particular, big cities traditionally based on manufacturing are diversifying into services and more likely to lead innovative new areas of production. Overall, the service sector has been growing considerably across Mexican cities and accounts for an increasing number of jobs and GVA, in particular in the MCMA. In big and medium cities, the service sector has also expanded quickly, from 10 and 14 percent of GVA in 1990, respectively, to nearly a quarter of productive activity in 2010, although big cities continue to be important poles for manufacturing (figure 2.4a and 2.4b). In addition, a ranking by the Mexican Institute for Competitiveness (*Instituto Mexicano para la Competitividad*, IMCO) in 2014 indicates that large cities with populations of more than 1 million inhabitants are among the cities with the highest current innovation in economic sectors.[2]

The shift in economic structure of Mexican cities is also reflected in the extent of economic specialization. An analysis of the Herfindahl-Hirschman Index suggests that medium and big cities with populations between 500,000 and 1 million diversified their economic bases between 1990 and 2010, whereas the MCMA became more specialized between 1990 and 2010 (figure 2.5). Economic activities in small cities remain specialized.

Remaining Challenges in Realizing the Full Economic Potential of Mexican Cities

Despite continued urbanization and associated economic growth, productivity in Mexico has been lagging behind its potential in part because the benefits from agglomeration have not been captured. Overall productivity in Mexico, as measured by the GVA per worker, grew just from 253 pesos per worker in 1990 to 272 pesos in 2010.[3] The 2000s had more productivity growth, in part to make up the losses from the recession of the late 1990s. Nonetheless, Mexico's productivity growth lags behind many of its peers in the region and countries of similar levels of urbanization internationally (figure 2.6). Further, growth in productivity has been uneven, and differences between leading and lagging regions have sharpened. This has real consequences: low productivity is responsible for halving the overall GDP per capita growth in the last decade (OECD 2013).

Several factors are known to contribute to the lack of productivity and innovation in Mexican cities. Mexico remains a country of small businesses, many of which operate in the informal sector. Between 1999 and 2009, microbusinesses, with fewer than 10 employees, were the only category of firms to lose productivity (Bolio 2014). But because microbusinesses are numerous, making up more than 90 percent of manufacturing enterprises and nearly half of employment, the costs of informality and size are significant for the economy on the whole (Bolio 2014; OECD 2013). Regulatory barriers, labor inflexibility, poor

Figure 2.4 Economic Composition of Mexican Cities by City Size, 1990 and 2010

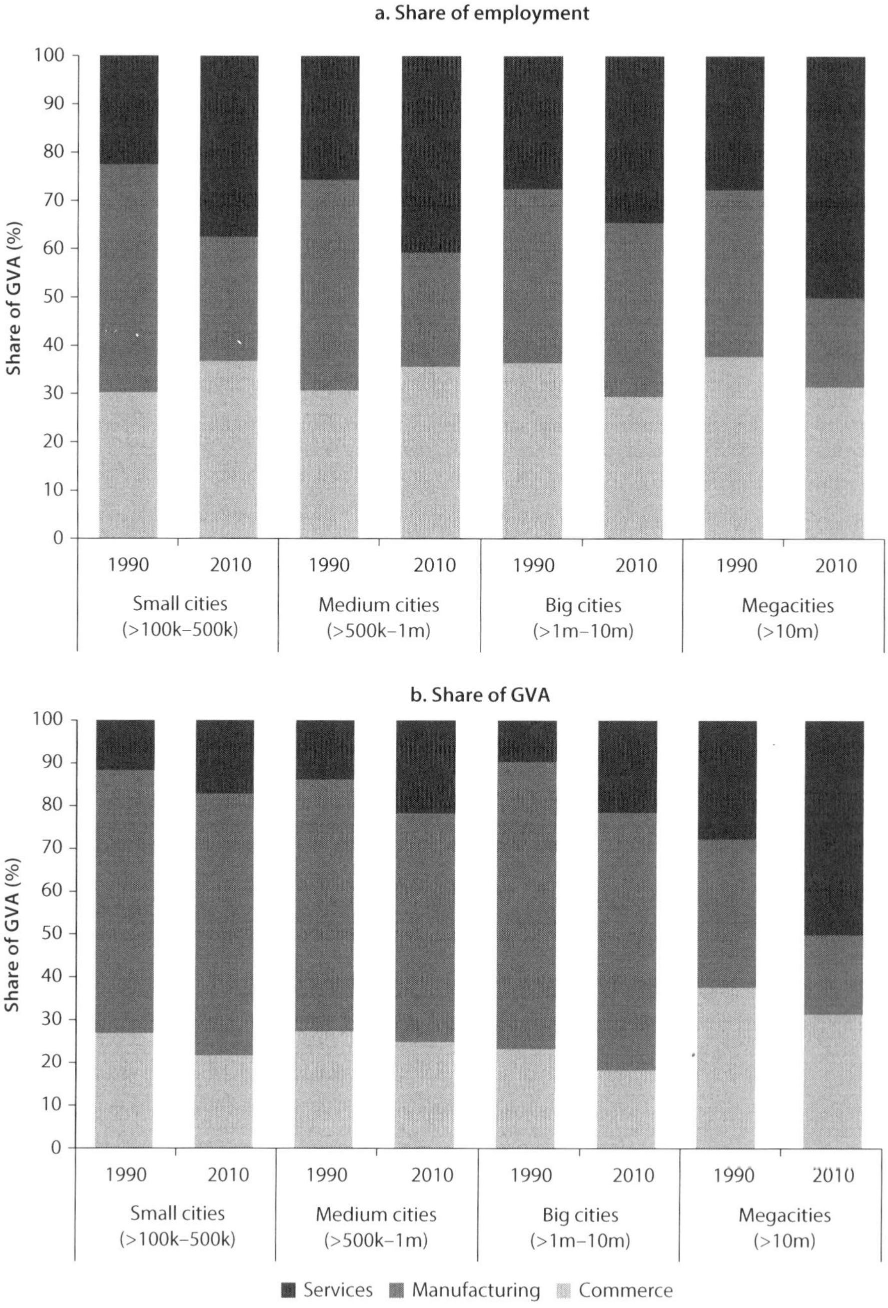

a. Share of employment

b. Share of GVA

■ Services ■ Manufacturing ▒ Commerce

Source: World Bank analysis based on economic census data from the National Institute of Statistics and Geography (*Instituto Nacional de Estadística y Geografía*, INEGI).
Note: The mining sector was excluded from the analysis because the methodology to attribute GVA from mining to particular municipalities changed between 1990 and 2010. The largest share of GVA from mining is generated in smaller cities. GVA = gross value added.

Figure 2.5 Sectoral Specialization and Diversity by City Size, 1990 and 2010

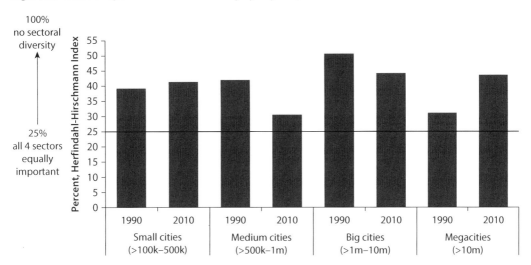

Source: World Bank analysis based on economic census data from the National Institute of Statistics and Geography (*Instituto Nacional de Estadística y Geografía,* INEGI).
Note: GVA = gross value added.

Figure 2.6 Productivity Growth per Capita, 1960–2005

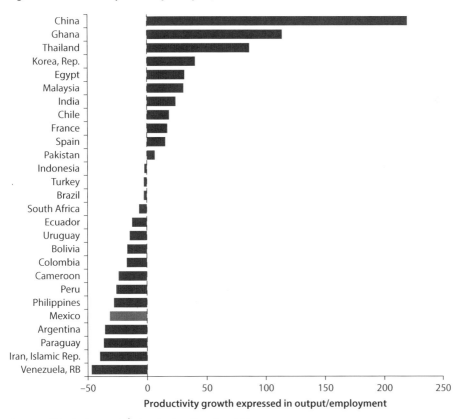

Source: World Bank adaptation based on data from Páges-Serra 2010.
Note: Using the United States as a baseline (=0).

educational attainments, and associated issues with quality of labor and weak institutions also present challenges to unlocking productivity across sectors (McMillan and Rodrik 2011; OECD 2013).

But place also matters for business. How cities grow, expand infrastructure and connectivity, and unlock agglomeration economies can also play a significant role in shaping their productive potential. Unfettered expansion comes with costs. Recent research found that the U.S. economy loses US$1 trillion yearly because of costs associated with sprawl (Litman 2015). But constraining development is not the solution alone: another study presents a different story—US$1 trillion yearly in missed GDP growth due to growth restrictions on high-performing cities (Hsieh and Moretti 2014). Decision-making structures and coordination make a difference as well; an OECD global review (2015) suggests that doubling the number of municipalities in an urban area of any given size correlated with a 6 percent lower relative productivity, whereas the presence of metropolitan governance entities was associated with a 3 percent higher productivity compared to other cities.

Progress and Remaining Challenges to Inclusive Growth in the Urban Sphere

As in other countries around the world, urbanization in Mexico has been associated with increased prosperity and reduced poverty. The average real household labor income in cities with more than 100,000 inhabitants increased significantly across all cities between 1990 and 2010. The increase was sharpest in big cities, where average household income nearly quadrupled from Mex$209,000 in 1990 to Mex$774,000 in 2010, reaching the highest average income levels among all city size groups (see figure 2.7). Similarly, income poverty levels have decreased across all city groups between 1990 and 2010, with the most significant reductions in medium cities. Generally, smaller cities have lower household incomes and higher poverty rates than larger cities. For example, when looking at food poverty, all city types show lower poverty rates in 2010 than in 1990, but at 16 percent, food poverty remains higher in small cities vis-à-vis all other city types where food poverty was 13.8 percent in 2010 (see figure 2.8; for details on poverty measures in Mexico see box 2.2).

Despite increased economic prosperity, Mexican cities continue to host a large number of the country's poor and extreme poverty remains a challenge, particularly in the southern region as well as in Mexico City. Although poverty rates have historically been lower in cities than in rural areas, in absolute terms, most of Mexico's poor actually live in urban areas. In 2010, there were about 52 million poor people in the country (measured in multidimensional poverty; see box 2.2), including 35 million in urban areas. Looking at extreme poverty, the picture is somewhat different with the higher concentration of extremely poor living in rural areas. Nonetheless, about 5.5 million urban poor continue to live in extreme poverty. As can be seen in figure 2.8a, it is striking that not only smaller cities but also the megalopolis Mexico City fared worse than big cities in

Figure 2.7 Household Labor Income and Food Poverty by City Size, 1990 and 2010

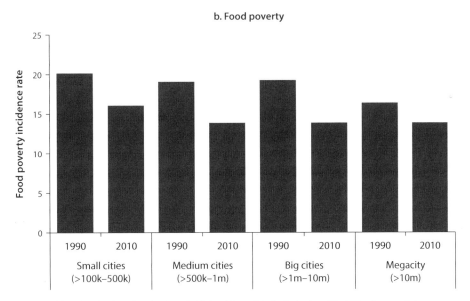

a. Real household labor income
(constant at 1990 Mex$, in thousands)

Source: World Bank analysis based on data from the National Institute of Statistics and Geography (*Instituto Nacional de Estadística y Geografía*, INEGI).

b. Food poverty

Source: World Bank analysis based on data from the National Council for the Evaluation of Social Development Policy (CONEVAL).

terms of extreme poverty in 2010. In terms of food access deficit, Mexico City scores even worse compared to all other city size groups.[4] Figure 2.8b also shows that extreme poverty and high food access deficits are concentrated in cities in the southern and, to a lesser extent, central region of Mexico, whereas cities located in the north and border regions are comparatively well off.

Figure 2.8 Extreme Poverty and Food Access Deficit by City Size and Region, 2010

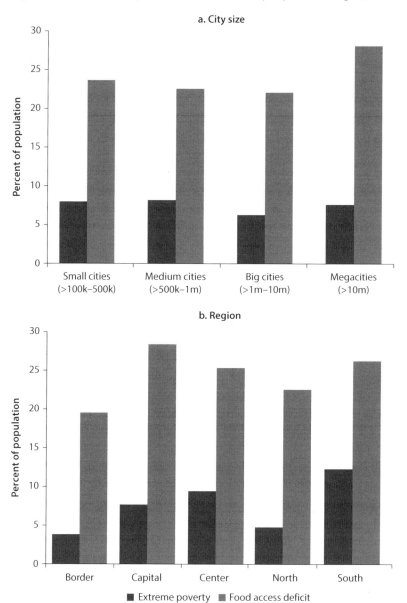

Source: World Bank analysis based on data from the National Council for the Evaluation of Social Development Policy (*Consejo Nacional de Evaluación de la Política de Desarrollo Social,* CONEVAL).

Despite some improvements, inequality remains relatively high across all city types and slightly more pronounced in the south. On average, the 100 largest Mexican cities became more equal measured by the Gini coefficient over the past two decades, despite having experienced increases in income inequality between 1990 and 2000.[5] Figure 2.9 shows that small and medium cities with

Box 2.2 Poverty Measures Used in Mexico

Poverty is commonly measured by income. *Income poverty* refers to the percentage of the population without the monetary resources to obtain basic goods and services, as required within their social environment. Although some of these goods and services are provided by the public sector, most need to be purchased by households. Populations without an adequate level of income to obtain the basic basket of goods and services are considered to be at a disadvantage compared with other members of their society. Mexico's National Council for the Evaluation of Social Development Policy (*Consejo Nacional de Evaluación de la Política de Desarrollo Social*, CONEVAL), the institution responsible for calculating poverty measures at the national, state, and municipal levels, uses three different measures to express income poverty (CONEVAL 2010a, 2010b):

1. *Food poverty*, which measures the share of the population that, even when using all of their income on basic food, are not able to afford the minimum required for adequate nutrition.
2. *Poverty based on capacities*, which measures the share of the population that cannot cover an adequate food basket and health and education expenses, even when using all of their income.
3. *Poverty based on assets*, which measures the share of the population that cannot cover an adequate food basket or expenses on education, health, clothes, shoes, property, and transportation, even when using all their income.

In addition to these income poverty measures, CONEVAL also measures *multidimensional poverty*, which takes into account both economic well-being and social rights. Economic well-being is assessed by comparing per capita income with a poverty line that defines a minimum threshold of monetary resources required for consumption to satisfy basic needs. The social rights dimension is evaluated using a social deprivation index that is constructed as the sum of six indicators: (i) access to food, (ii) quality and space of housing, (iii) access to basic services in the dwelling, (iv) access to health services, (v) educational gap, and (vi) access to social security. Those people with income below the economic well-being threshold that suffer at least one social deprivation are considered to be multidimensionally poor.

Extreme poverty is defined based on the calculations for multidimensional poverty and food poverty. People are considered to be extremely poor when they experience two conditions: (i) they suffer at least three of the six social deprivations, and (ii) even spending the totality of their income on food, they are unable to achieve the caloric intake required for a healthy lifestyle.

CONEVAL also measures the *food access deficit* as an indicator for poverty. This deficit is based on the right of individuals to access adequate food and on the minimum level of food needed for adequate nutrition. In order to have a measure that reflects the limitations of the right to adequate nutrition, the calculation considers households with some degree of food insecurity. The degree of food insecurity reflects the lack of caloric intake, considering first adults and then children.

Figure 2.9 Gini Coefficient by City Size Type and Region, 1990 and 2010

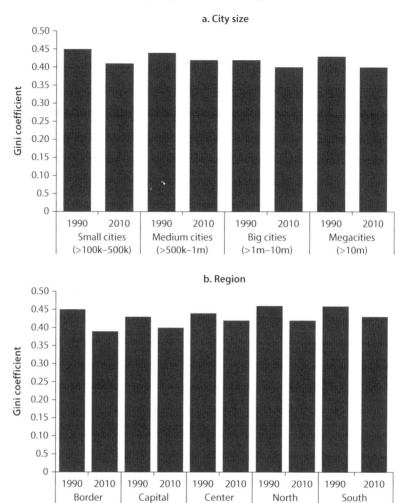

Source: World Bank analysis based on data from the National Council for the Evaluation of Social Development Policy (*Consejo Nacional de Evaluación de la Política de Desarrollo Social* CONEVAL).

populations between 100,000 and 1 million have slightly higher levels of inequality in terms of income than do larger cities. In regional comparison, the highest inequality is found in cities in the south, whereas cities in the border region achieved the greatest improvements in terms of income inequality. Generally speaking, differences in terms of inequality across cities and regions were rather small in 2010, but with values over 0.4 Gini coefficients remain high in international comparison.

Human development also increased across all city types and regions, but challenges remain, particularly regarding education. The positive trends in terms of reductions in poverty and inequality in recent decades were accompanied by further improvements in human development. Figure 2.10 shows that the

Figure 2.10 Human Development Index by City Size and Region, 1995 and 2005

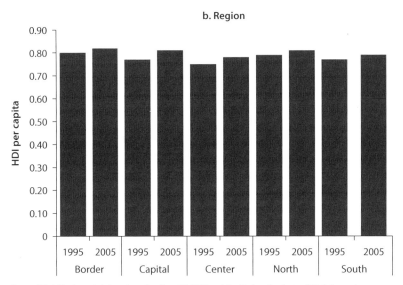

a. City size

b. Region

Source: World Bank analysis based on data from SIMBAD and the National Institute of Statistics and Geography (*Instituto Nacional de Estadística y Geografía,* INEGI).
Note: HDI = Human Development Index.

Human Development Index (HDI)[6] further improved from already high levels in 1995 for all city size groups to reach the tier of very high human development in large cities and Mexico City in 2005. Regional differences in terms of human development are small but persistent; although cities in the southern and central regions continue to have the lowest HDIs among Mexican cities, border and

Figure 2.11 Education Attainment by City Size, 1990 and 2010

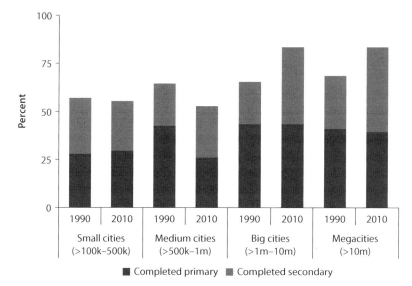

Source: World Bank analysis based on data from the National Institute of Statistics and Geography (*Instituto Nacional de Estadística y Geografía*, INEGI).

northern cities have managed to transition to very high HDIs. However, Mexican cities show mixed results in terms of educational indicators. While the number of people who complete secondary education has nearly doubled in big cities and Mexico City between 1990 and 2010, education attainments in smaller cities remain low (see figure 2.11).

Mexican cities are not immune to national and regional trends of crime and violence and, in recent years, citizen security has worsened in many Mexican cities. There has been a significant increase in the rate of intentional homicides and kidnappings across all city size groups and regions since 2007 when the government began implementing the war against organized crime. Whereas homicide rates are much higher in medium, big, and small cities, Mexico City has higher rates of kidnappings. The number of homicides has decreased slightly in big and medium cities since 2010 but remains at levels three times higher than those of 2007. From a regional perspective, the biggest growth of intentional homicides since 2007 took place in border and northern cities—areas used for drug trafficking to the United States. Robberies seem to be more frequent in smaller and medium-size cities and in northern cities (where they also increased most drastically compared to 2006) and cities in the central region.[7]

Recent Spatial Growth and Its Impact on Mexican Cities

Widespread and rapid horizontal expansion of built-up area has drastically changed the spatial form of Mexican cities in recent decades. Between 1980 and 2010, the built-up area of Mexican cities has on average expanded by a factor of seven, and the urbanized area of the 11 biggest metropolitan areas with more than 1 million inhabitants in 2010 has even grown by a factor of nine (SEDESOL 2012). As revealed by the National Housing Program (*Programa Nacional de Vivienda*, PNV), expansion toward the periphery in the past has overwhelmingly occurred without clearly demarcated planning guidelines, boundaries for growth, design, and zoning clusters (SEGOB 2013).

This substantial change in urban form traces back to housing policies that favored the massive construction of single-use horizontal housing developments on the outskirts of cities, without concomitant urban planning. The expansion of Mexican cities has largely been an unintentional effect of changes in housing policy that aimed to reduce housing deficits, with limited attention to the overall functionality and accessibility of newly built urban areas. As a result of housing policy reform and aided by macroeconomic stability, over 7 million new low-cost housing units were built between 2006 and 2011, most of which are individual, single-story houses in peri-urban areas. The resulting sprawl of Mexican cities is different from suburbanization in the United States during the 1960s and 1970s, where middle-class households moved to suburbs for more space with better amenities and schools. Instead, urban growth in Mexico has been connected to the fissure between new, peri-urban developments and more central neighborhoods in terms of the provision of infrastructure and services (including health and education), connectivity, access to sources of employment, and urban amenities.

The recent pattern of urbanization in Mexico appears to underutilize the potential of cities to spark innovation, boost economic growth, and foster social inclusion. Large cities account for much of Mexico's economic output and have contributed to poverty reduction, yet their economic performance could be even better and inequality remains an important challenge despite ongoing urbanization. To transition into an upper-middle-income country, more could be done to unlock the potential of Mexican cities to nurture inclusive growth. The following chapters will explore the links between spatial form of Mexican cities, their economic performance, and their livability.

Notes

1. INEGI measures sector production by gross value added (GVA), which is equivalent to sector GDP plus product subsidies and minus product direct and sales taxes.

2. Out of the 79 cities ranked in 2014, just six cities received a score of 30 or above, out of a possible total of 100, indicating higher levels of innovation and competitiveness. Of those, four had populations above 1 million inhabitants (IMCO 2014).

3. All GVA numbers are presented in real pesos from 2012. The GVA is a measure of the values of goods and services produced in an area or sector of the economy. GVA is related to GDP because both measure output. However, GVA does not include taxes and subsidies on products, which GDP does. Measurements of the GVA in this review are weighted by the workforce (L) in that municipality for every period.

4. According to CONEVAL, this may be explained by the hike in food prices resulting from the economic crisis of 2007, which hit households in Mexico City harder as the price level in the capital was already higher than in the rest of the country.

5. According to CONEVAL statistics, the higher Gini coefficient in 2000 could be explained by the economic crisis of 1994, which affected mostly the vulnerable populations in each city, increasing the income inequality within cities.

6. The HDI is a summary of measure of average achievement in key dimensions of human development, including life expectancy, education, and decent standard of living that is produced by the United Nations Development Program (UNDP). The HDI is the geometric mean of normalized indexes for each of these dimensions and ranges between 0 and 1. Based on the results, countries are ranked into four tiers of human development: very high (>0.8), high (0.7–0.8), medium (0.55–0.7), and low (<0.55).

7. Spatially disaggregated data on crime and violence within municipalities is not available in Mexico. Hence, it was not possible to analyze the impact of urban form on crime and violence within cities.

References

Ahrend, Rudiger, Emily Farchy, Ioannis Kaplanis, and Alexander C. Lembcke. 2014. "What Makes Cities More Productive? Evidence on the Role of Urban Governance from Five OECD Countries." OECD Regional Development Working Papers 2014/05, OECD, Paris. doi: http://dx.doi.org/10.1787/5jz432cf2d8p-en.

Bolio, E. 2014. *A Tale of Two Mexicos: Growth and Prosperity in a Two-Speed Economy.* McKinsey Global Institute.

Ciccone, A., and R. E. Hall.1993. "Productivity and the Density of Economic Activity." NBER Working Paper 4313, National Bureau of Economic Research, Cambridge MA.

CONEVAL (*Consejo Nacional de Evaluación de la Política de Desarrollo Social*). 2010a. *La pobreza por ingresos en México.* Mexico City, Mexico: CONEVAL.

————. 2010b. *Methodology for Multidimensional Poverty Measurement in Mexico. An Executive Version.* Mexico City, Mexico: CONEVAL.

Glaeser, Edward L., Hedi D. Kallal, José A. Scheinkman, and Andrei Shleifer. 1992. "Growth in Cities." *Journal of Political Economy* 100: 1126–52.

Hsieh, C.-T., and E. Moretti. 2014. "Growth in Cities and Countries." 2014 National Bureau of Economic Research (NBER) Session on Economic Growth, Cambridge, MA.

IMCO (*Instituto Mexicano para la Competitividad*). 2014. Índice de Competitividad Urbana 2014. ¿Quién manda aquí? La gobernanza de las ciudades y el territorio en México. Mexico City, Mexico: IMCO. http://imco.org.mx/indices/documentos/2014 _ICU_Libro_La_gobernanza_de_las_ciudades_y_el_territorio_en_Mexico.pdf.

Litman, T. 2015. *Analysis of Public Policies that Unintentionally Encourage and Subsidize Urban Sprawl.* London: New Climate Economy, Global Commission on the Economy and Climate.

McMillan, M. S., and D. Rodrik. 2011. "Globalization, Structural Change and Productivity Growth." NBER Working Paper 17143, National Bureau of Economic Research, Cambridge, MA.

OECD (Organisation for Economic Co-operation and Development). 2013. *OECD Economic Surveys: Mexico 2013.* Paris: OECD.

————. 2015. *The Metropolitan Century, Understanding Urbanization and Its Consequences.* Paris: OECD.

Páges-Serra, Carmen. 2010. *The Age of Productivity: Transforming Economies from the Bottom Up*. Washington, DC: Inter-American Development Bank.

Rosenthal, S. S., and W. C. Strange. 2004. "Evidence on the Nature and Sources of Agglomeration Economies." In *Handbook of Regional and Urban Economics: Cities and Geography*, Vol. 4, edited by J. Vernon Henderson and Jacques-François Thisse. Amsterdam: Elsevier.

SEDESOL (*Secretariat de Desarrollo Social*). 2012. *La expansión de las ciudades 1980–2010*. Mexico City, Mexico: SEDESOL.

SEGOB (*Secretaría de Gobernación*). 2013. *Programa Nacional de Vivienda*. Mexico City, Mexico: SEGOB.

Storper, M., and A. J. Venables. 2004. "Buzz: Face-to-Face Contact and The Urban Economy." *Journal of Economic Geography* 4 (4): 351–70.

World Bank. 2009. *World Development Report 2009: Reshaping Economic Geography*. Washington, DC:World Bank.

———. 2015. *World Development Indicators*. Washington, DC: World Bank. http://data .worldbank.org/data-catalog/world-development-indicators.

CHAPTER 3

Unlocking the Economic Potentials of Mexican Cities

Introduction

The prevailing urban growth pattern of Mexican cities has affected their ability to take advantage of urban agglomeration to match skills and jobs, efficiently sort activities within the urban area, and encourage spillover effects. The spatial dimension is by no means the only factor that determines the economic performance of a city, but urban form does lay the groundwork for cities to fulfill certain functions that can boost economic growth. If a city has a spatial structure that facilitates matching of skills to jobs, manages to distribute economic and other activities evenly throughout the urban area, and creates economic densities that foster agglomeration economies and knowledge spillovers, then its economy is likely to thrive.

Spatial dynamics of cities influence the distance between people and employment, and can also affect the ability of people to connect with one another and the government's capacity to equip properly an entire urban area with infrastructure and services. Firms, in particular skill-intensive industries, choose to settle in particular locations considering aspects such as land prices, access to workers, and transport costs. Firms may have reduced access to workers with specific skill sets in sprawling cities, in particular if these suffer from lagging transportation services, long commuting times, congestion, and high transportation costs. In addition, long distances between homes and jobs in the absence of adequate connective infrastructure can prevent workers from accessing suitable jobs and interacting with other skilled workers. The shorter the distance and the lower the transportation costs, the higher the opportunities for interactions between workers and firms, resulting in knowledge diffusion (Glaeser et al. 1992).

This chapter analyzes the spatial dynamic of Mexican cities in recent years with regard to its potential impacts on economic performance. It will first examine how the recent peri-urban expansion influences the distance and connectivity between housing and jobs, revealing shortcomings in the sorting of activities across space and affecting cities' ability to match skills with jobs. It will then

assess to what extent Mexican cities reap the benefits of agglomeration economies. Last, it will also look at the effects of sprawl on providing infrastructure and
at how metropolitan coordination could help urban areas to unlock their potential. Although only a first step, the chapter establishes basic analysis upon which
further research can examine more sophisticated mechanisms underlying
Mexico's low urban productivity.

Effects of Uncoordinated Urban Growth on Matching Skills to Jobs

While overall population density of Mexican cities did not change much in
recent decades, density dynamics *within* the cities have changed considerably,
resulting in two noticeable trends. First, there has been a considerable drop in the
number of people living in city centers. Between 2000 and 2010, 67 of the
91 largest cities lost population in their central two kilometers. Eighteen of these
cities lost more than 20 percent of their central city population.[1] This trend is
not limited to smaller or less dynamic cities; Hermosillo, Léon, Matamoros,
Monterrey, Puebla, and Queretaro were among the cities that experienced a
significant population loss in the city center.

The second trend that stands out in Mexican cities of all sizes is an increase of
population densities in peripheral neighborhoods. This results primarily from the
push to build low-cost housing and is different from the traditional form of urban
sprawl, which is characterized by low-density residential development
(Monkkonen 2011). The construction boom of horizontal housing since the
2000s, which has largely been driven by changes in housing policies, has successfully enhanced the access to affordable housing and substantially contributed to
gross domestic product (GDP). However, the new housing developments are
often situated in peri-urban communities far away from the economic activities
of the central cities and thus distant from job opportunities. The density gradient
for the Queretaro Metropolitan Area in figure 3.1 shows the decline in population densities in central areas of the city and increasing densities in areas that are
over 2.5 kilometers away from the city center.

The recent trends of hollowing city centers and expanding urban peripheries are accompanied by an increasing number of housing vacancies in inner
cities. Lower population density in city centers may not be a problem in itself
and is observed in many cities in the United States when the inner cities
serve mainly as providers of economic activities and employment. In the case
of Mexican cities, however, the hollowing city centers are characterized by
underused urban cores often accompanied by a high number of vacant houses.
Table 3.1 shows the average share of vacant housing in the inner city and peri-
urban parts of the 100 largest cities in Mexico in two different ways. The first
is the average vacancy rate for census tracts in the inner city and urban periphery. The second is the share of the city's vacant housing located in the inner
city and urban periphery. Although on average the vacancy rate is higher in
the peri-urban parts of the city, inner city areas have on average a much larger
share of these cities' vacant housing (Monkkonen 2014). Map 3.1 shows this

Figure 3.1 Shifting Population Densities in Queretaro, 1990–2010

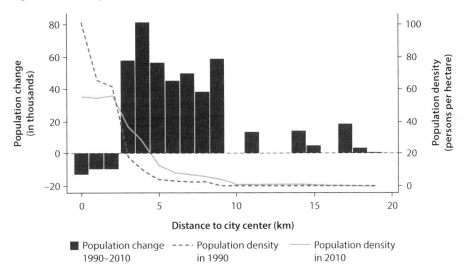

Source: World Bank analysis based on data from the National Institute of Statistics and Geography (*Instituto Nacional de Estadística y Geografía*, INEGI).

Table 3.1 Share of Vacant Housing in the Inner City and Peri-Urban Areas of the 100 Largest Cities in Mexico

	Vacancy rate[a]		Share of city's vacant housing[b]	
	Percent	Standard Deviation	Percent	Standard Deviation
Inner city	12.8	3.0	32.8	7.7
Peri-urban	16.3	6.0	19.8	7.6

Source: Monkkonen 2014.

a. The *vacancy rate* is defined as vacant housing in a particular area of the city divided by the total housing in that same area of the city (for example, vacant housing in the inner city divided by the total housing in the inner city).

b. The *share of a city's vacant housing* is defined as vacant housing in a particular area of the city divided by the total housing for the city (for example, vacant housing in the inner city divided by total housing in the entire city).

trend for the example of the Mérida Metropolitan Area, where the overall vacancy rate was 15 percent in 2010 (compared to an average of 14 percent for the 100 largest Mexican cities). Although the vacancy rate was higher in the peri-urban area (21 percent) than in the inner city (13 percent), the share of vacant housing in the inner city was 29 percent versus 21 percent in the urban periphery.

Although people are moving farther away from city centers, jobs remain much more centralized, undermining cities' ability to match skills to jobs. Historically, cities tend to agglomerate their economic activities in the center, where infrastructure and services are well consolidated, and where population movement is highly dynamic. However, when populations move

Map 3.1 Housing Vacancy Rates in the Mérida Metropolitan Area

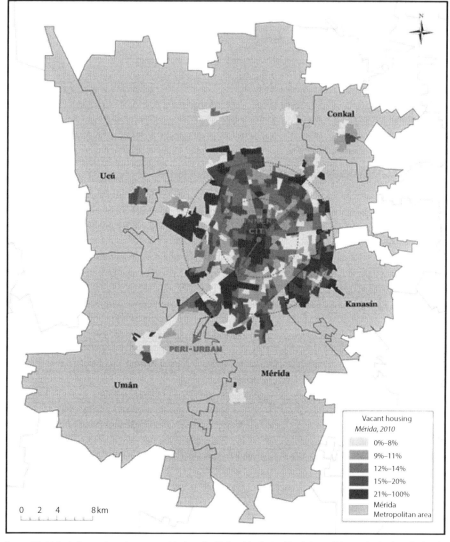

Source: World Bank diagram based on census data from the National Institute of Statistics and Geography *(Instituto Nacional de Estadística y Geografía,* INEGI).
Note: Categories in legend are quintiles. Vacancy rates of 100 percent may refer to brand new housing that had not yet been occupied at the time of data collection. The average housing vacancy rate in Mexican cities is 14 percent.

(or are forced to move) away from the city center to reside in the periphery, they lose accessibility to the economic centers of cities, including to jobs. Our analysis shows that jobs consistently have a much steeper density gradient than population does in Mexico.[2] Maps 3.2 and 3.3 and figure 3.2 provide a visual sense of the relatively inverse dynamic between population and job densities for the example of the Monterrey Metropolitan Area. Map 3.2 shows the variation in population densities within Monterrey, with people

Map 3.2 Distribution of Population in Monterrey, 2010

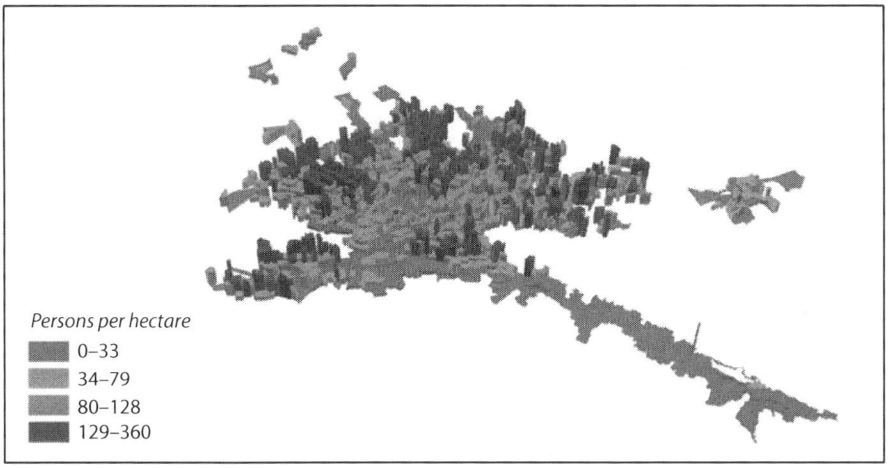

Persons per hectare
- 0–33
- 34–79
- 80–128
- 129–360

Source: World Bank analysis based on data from the National Institute of Statistics and Geography (*Instituto Nacional de Estadística y Geografía*, INEGI).

Map 3.3 Distribution of Jobs in Monterrey, 2010

Jobs per hectare
- 0–2
- 3–6
- 7–14
- 15–370

Source: World Bank analysis based on data from the National Institute of Statistics and Geography (*Instituto Nacional de Estadística y Geografía*, INEGI).
Note: Job density is shown by Basic Geostatistical Area/Census Tract (*Área Geoestadística Básica*). These are the equivalent of census tracts in other countries and roughly correspond to neighborhoods containing an average of 1,900 residents and covering 40 hectares.

concentrating on the outskirts of the city center while the city center hosts low population densities (mostly in green). In contrast, map 3.3 shows that higher job densities concentrate mostly in the center of Monterrey (darker brown). Bringing both trends together, figure 3.2 clearly shows that the highest number of jobs in 2010 (close to 100,000 jobs) were within 5 kilometers of the city center, while population has shifted further away from the city center over the past decades.

Mexico Urbanization Review • http://dx.doi.org/10.1596/978-1-4648-0916-3

Figure 3.2 Population and Job Density by Distance to City Center, Monterrey, 1990 and 2010

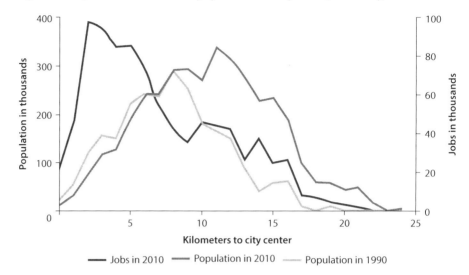

Source: World Bank diagram based on data from the National Institute of Statistics and Geography (Instituto Nacional de Estadística y Geografía, INEGI).
Note: There are no data available at the census tract level for 1990.

Effects of Uncoordinated Urban Growth on Sorting Economic Activities in Space

The distribution of residential and economic activities in Mexican cities could be rebalanced by incentivizing the creation of employment subcenters and the revitalization of dilapidated central areas into flourishing mixed-use neighborhoods. On the one hand, developments in suburban areas with multifunctional land use and full access to urban infrastructure can encourage firms to locate in different parts of the city. In particular, firms that need to build large facilities for their production operations may prefer to build their facilities outside the city center in suburban areas where land is cheaper and households can benefit from accessing closer jobs. Creating employment subcenters can help cities take advantage of activity clusters and agglomeration economies in expansion areas, which in Mexican cities are now predominantly used for housing; jobs remain located monocentrically, worsening burdens on commuting cost and time for both households and firms. On the other hand, promoting revitalization and redensification of the urban core, for instance by increasing the provision of affordable housing in inner cities, would also help to bring people—and in particular low-income populations—closer to their jobs. See box 3.1 for opportunities, challenges, and international experience with urban regeneration.

A metropolitan approach to policies, such as metro-level plans for expansion or subcenters, is needed to balance jobs and housing. Large metropolitan areas or conurbations can plan for the development of several subcenters with mixed land uses, within and outside the peripheral areas, which can serve as growth centers for the "overspill" of jobs and residents from the central city (Jones 2000)

Box 3.1 Urban Regeneration: Advantages, Bottlenecks, and International Practices

International experiences with urban regeneration and renewal illustrate a wide range of successes, in which small investments have yielded significant benefits. Urban renewal has shown to have positive effects on labor markets, in part because centrally located development reduces the distance between jobs and people, and can create the density needed for economies of agglomeration for firms to innovate. Public funding for services and basic infrastructure can be higher up front if significant rehabilitation of networks is needed, but over the long term, the funds required can be significantly lower than those needed for the comparable greenfield development. Placing new development in accessible and serviced areas can also be a powerful tool to increase equity and improve access to opportunity for low-income households.

Urban regeneration projects can be lengthy and difficult to implement (for example, complex land assembly, permitting, re-zoning processes, as well as financing and project management). However, successful experiences and techniques have been documented in cities across the world. While there is no one-size-fits-all model, policy makers must identify strategies for the two major prongs of any renewal project: (i) tools to capture the financial and land assets of the city and (ii) strategies for effective implementation.

Innovative tools can leverage the financial and land assets of cities to attract further investment to overcome financial and land assembly constraints. Johannesburg's recent experience with the Urban Development Zone (UDZ) tax incentives finds they are estimated to have attracted about US$300 million of private investment yearly to the center city, creating over 65,000 construction jobs and making housing available to the emerging middle class (Garner 2011). The incentive takes the form of a tax allowance that covers an accelerated depreciation of investment made in either refurbishment of existing property or the creation of new developments within the inner city, over five or seventeen years, respectively. Any taxpaying, property-owning individual or entity may claim the tax benefits of the UDZ incentive.[a]

Regulatory changes in density can also spur investment. New York City has used "density bonuses" to finance urban infrastructure provision. The city government entices private developers to participate in the provision of specific public purposes—including the improvement of infrastructure, creation of public spaces, development of affordable housing, preservation of historic sites, and so on—in exchange for additional development rights (building higher and more densely) in intense urban areas (Tiesdell and Adams 2011). The value of additional development granted would cover the costs of those public goods.

Public land can be exchanged in return for development through either long-term leases or a transfer of land ownership. Washington, DC, was able to restore the Anacostia Riverfront through a successful interagency partnership and land exchange that allowed the Government of the District of Columbia to redevelop 500 acres of waterfront land. The entire development has attracted US$1.8 billion in public investment coming from the District, local quasi-government corporations, and federal agencies, along with a US$7 billion investment from private entities (Government of the District of Columbia 2010). Land can also be used as equity for a joint stock redevelopment company, as in Buenos Aires with the *Corporación Antiguo Puerto Madero Sociedad Anónima*, where the various owners of land along the

box continues next page

Box 3.1 Urban Regeneration: Advantages, Bottlenecks, and International Practices *(continued)*

waterfront joined efforts to redevelop the city's old port. In both cases—Washington, DC, and Buenos Aires—urban regeneration came about through close cooperation of different government levels.

Coordination between government agencies, private investors, civil organizations, and other stakeholders is as critical for the success of urban regeneration projects as are the technical tools and the strategies for implementation. A shared scoping can lay the groundwork for an intentionally designed planning process that gives ample space, voice, and incentives for the multiple actors to contribute, whether through a government-established company (special purpose corporation [SPC] or special purpose vehicle [SPV]) or a public-private partnership. These components can be formalized into a regeneration area master plan that lays out rules of the game, financing strategy, and a physical plan with a vision for height, open space, environment, image, transport, and design (CABE 2008).

Finally, to avoid the trap of renewal projects becoming one-off and piecemeal projects, international experience points to the need for projects to focus on how to embed new processes within existing systems. By understanding the larger building blocks that have prevented investment in the first place, renewal initiatives can use their momentum to spread innovations and lessons-learned methods into institutions that work at scale and over the long term. In this way, the new methods developed, from effective community charrettes to zoning tools, can reach beyond the bounds of the project.

a. For more information, see the official website of the City of Johannesburg, www.joburg.org.za.

(see box 3.2 for the experience in the Republic of Korea). This policy can be realized only if the government is able to attract private investment (for example, public-private partnerships) needed for the construction of district centers and coordinate governance, investment, and service provision among municipalities. This approach would also require strengthened federal, state, and local efforts to identify appropriate locations for development to occur, to invest in the infrastructure needed for these developments at the metropolitan level, to enhance legal and regulatory regimes to deter irregular settlements, and to create the financial incentives for homebuyers and developers to support more sustainable housing. Moreover, spatial development policies at the metropolitan regional scale can be an effective mechanism to contain urban sprawl.

Missing Benefits from Agglomeration Economies in Mexican Cities

In addition to efficiently sorting activities across space and matching skills to jobs, urban spatial form and connectivity within cities can foster knowledge spillover effects that in turn can help boost economic performance. Firms that are associated with high-value economic activities benefit from having easy access to skilled workers and being close to other high value-added firms (OECD 2007). Cities, by bringing large numbers of people and firms together, facilitate the production of technical and organizational knowledge. Urban

Box 3.2 Reducing Overcrowding, Supplying Housing in Large-Scale Developments, and Creating Sustainable Cities through Subcenters: The Case of New Towns in the Republic of Korea

The Republic of Korea experienced an industrialization and urbanization wave in the 1960s and 1970s that led to severe housing shortages in cities in the following decades. In response to these challenges, the Korean government designed and implemented large-scale urban development projects, so-called "new towns," which evolved from residential towns into more complex urban centers. These large and complex projects were successful in achieving the government's goals to redistribute urban populations, to provide housing for low-income populations, and to create sustainable living environments. Their success lies on various integrated factors, including the creation of implementing institutions, legal support, a comprehensive urban planning system with mandatory guidelines for long-term urban planning, and political will to cooperate at local, county, and national levels toward a common urban vision.

The severe housing shortage, high population growth, and housing deficiencies of the 1980s led public authorities to design the first-generation residential towns. Five new towns with 292,000 residential units for more than 1.1 million inhabitants were built and financed by the government. Located on government-purchased land in the surroundings of Seoul, these towns shared three common features: (i) a commuting time to Seoul of up to an hour, facilitated by better transportation services and improved metropolitan transportation networks throughout the capital area; (ii) connections to urban infrastructure systems; and (iii) pleasant-looking built environments, with high rates of open space (ranging from 13 to 21 percent) and access to community facilities. Of the housing units built within this plan, 42.5 percent were designated for public housing, 24 percent for rental housing, and 33.5 percent for private housing. The first-generation new towns contributed to stabilizing the prices of real estate around the capital area, by supplying a large number of residential units. Even though the residential units targeted all income classes, 67.5 percent were occupied by low-income families. In terms of drawbacks, this initiative was believed to have accelerated the population concentration in the capital area, leading to excessively high densities, traffic congestion, price increase, and environmental destruction (due to extensive development).

In the 2000s, the government started implementing second-generation new towns to disperse urban populations and serve multiple (specific) purposes in an integrated manner—besides providing homes—such as accommodating administrative functions, building company towns, creating innovative urban centers, and offering pleasant living environments. The Korean government implemented a national territory development framework based on a "plan first, develop later" principle to encourage the development of city master plans with clear indications on infrastructure, location, and environmental guidelines. Thirteen new towns have been constructed since 2001. These new towns attempted to address the criticism of the previous generation of new towns and pursue environmental, social, and economic sustainability. Most of these new towns consisted of the redevelopment of old premises into vertical housing. Second-generation new towns were designed to have various types of density development, an increased park area ratio of 25–35 percent of the total urban area (10–12.5 percent higher than in first-generation new towns), advanced urban planning and

box continues next page

Box 3.2 Reducing Overcrowding, Supplying Housing in Large-Scale Developments, and Creating Sustainable Cities through Subcenters: The Case of New Towns in the Republic of Korea *(continued)*

design techniques (such as green network, ecology parks, waterways, and mixed-use development), and new transportation modes, including bus rapid transit (BRT), bicycle paths, trams, and pedestrian-friendly streetscapes. In terms of social and cultural structure, second-generation new towns aimed for a social mix, by connecting rental and for-sale housing in the residential layouts.

An important innovation to this generation of new towns is the stronger participation of local governments and private developers. Private developers acquire land, build, and sell the housing units while the public sector focuses on basic development planning and provision of basic infrastructure. A challenge of this new model is the limited investment of private entities with many new towns being launched simultaneously. In addition, the number of designated districts for new town development, as well as the large areas of designated spaces, has contributed to a real estate price hike and a slowdown in implementation. Nonetheless, second-generation new towns have helped manage the drastic population increase in Korean urban areas and achieve a balanced national development.

---

economy research has found that high densities and agglomeration allow ideas to spread and grow among people in close proximity (Jaffe, Trajtenberg, and Henderson 1993), increasing productivity (Lucas and Rossi-Handberg 2002). In particular, high value-added firms seek to locate in large urban centers where they can gain learning from many other types of high value-added firms (knowledge spillover).

In Mexico, the advantages of city size do not appear to be fully captured. The concentration of high value-added activities in large cities as described above follows international experience suggesting that megacities and large urban agglomerations can become nurseries for innovative activities and niche products especially in the high value-added service industry. However, compared internationally, Mexican cities appear to benefit only weakly from increased size and agglomeration economics to achieve higher levels of productivity, particularly Mexico City (OECD 2013; OECD 2015b).[3]

On the upside, there has been an increase in high value-added manufacturing activities. Even though the overall importance of the manufacturing sector in the economic structure of these cities has started to slowly decline, it has been moving toward higher value-added industries in small, medium, and large cities between 2000 and 2010 (figure 3.3). Data for Mexican cities show that low value-added manufacturing activities have declined in all city types during those ten years—slightly more in small and medium cities (4–5 percentage points in the former, as opposed to 2 percentage points in the latter). Medium value-added manufacturing activities have gone down only in small cities (2 percent), whereas high-value activities have grown more in small and medium cities (5 percent)

Figure 3.3 Composition of the Manufacturing Sector by City Size, 2000 and 2010

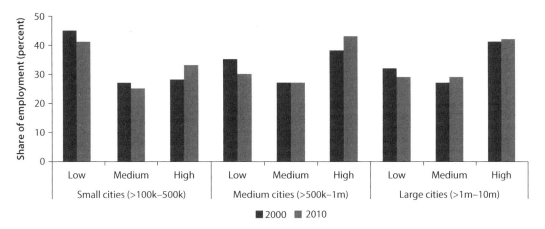

Source: World Bank analysis based on economic census data from the National Institute of Statistics and Geography *(Instituto Nacional de Estadística y Geografía,* INEGI).

than in big cities (1 percent). Overall, the manufacturing sector has achieved considerable productivity increases, in particular in small cities.

However, rapid expansion of the service sector in Mexican cities has failed to translate into high value-added activities and has stagnated into low-value service sectors. The labor market and productive focus of Mexican urban areas have pivoted in the last two decades to the service sector. However, in contrast to many peer countries, large cities in Mexico have not significantly expanded their high value-added service industries, such as finance, telecommunications, technology design, and insurance. Instead, data show that, between 2000 and 2010, low value-added service activities have taken up more than 60 percent of the service sector in small, medium, and big cities, and more than 50 percent in megacities (figure 3.4). High value-added service sector activities are mostly present in megacities, but have experienced a decline of five percentage points between 2000 and 2010 (from 36 percent to 31 percent); this difference seems to have shifted to low value-added activities—which experienced a six percent increase. Overall, the rapid growth of service sector jobs in Mexican cities concentrates in low-wage and low-productivity employment across all city sizes.

In particular, the Mexico City Metropolitan Area (MCMA) illustrates this missed opportunity of the economic transition—the city's rapid growth in the service sector has not maximized the benefits of agglomeration economies. Over the last quarter-century, the MCMA dramatically changed from a predominantly manufacturing-driven economy to services. Now, the service sector accounts for half of all formal employment and produces nearly 60 percent of the city's gross value added (GVA), quadruple the value of 15 percent in 1990. However, despite productivity increases, nearly all of that growth has pooled at the lowest value-added tier. Low value-added service activities expanded and now account for 54 percent of jobs in the service sector, whereas the share of high value-added activities has been declining

Figure 3.4 Composition of the Service Sector by City Size, 2000 and 2010

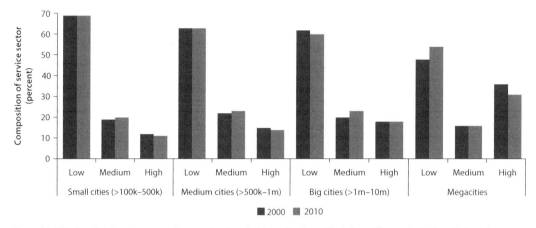

Source: World Bank analysis based on economic census data from the National Institute of Statistics and Geography (*Instituto Nacional de Estadística y Geografía,* INEGI).

Figure 3.5 Population Centralization and Service Sector Productivity, 1990 and 2010

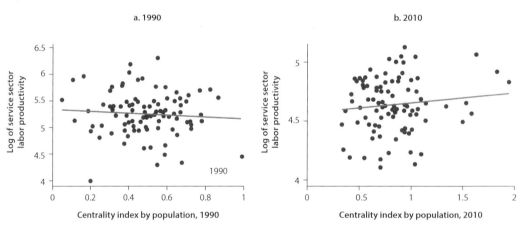

Source: World Bank calculation of centrality index based on data from the National Institute of Statistics and Geography (*Instituto Nacional de Estadística y Geografía,* INEGI) 1990 and 2010.
Note: The centrality index is the sum of inverse AGEB distances weighted by population. The graphs do not include outliers (one in 1990 and two in 2010). AGEB = Basic Geostatistical Area/Census Tract (*Área Geoestadística Básica*).

since 2010 (figure 3.5). Moreover, Mexico City also lags behind in terms of production per capita; it is not among the ten cities in the country with the highest GVA per capita.[4] This suggests Mexico City has not yet realized its full economic potential compared to other large metropolitan areas in the country, most notably Monterrey and Hermosillo.

The productivity gains in the service sector seem to concentrate in dense and centralized areas, as well as in cities in the north. An analysis of municipalities

Figure 3.6 Population Density and Manufacturing Productivity

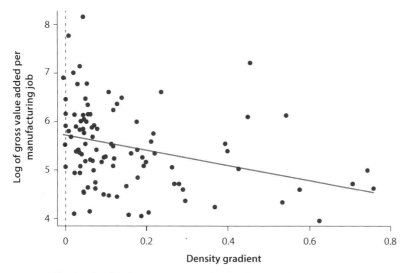

Source: World Bank analysis based on economic census data from the National Institute of Statistics and Geography *(Instituto Nacional de Estadística y Geografía,* INEGI).

across Mexico conducted for this review suggests that the relationship between service sector productivity and population centralization was negative in 1990. By 2010, the relationship shifted; and, although weak, population centralization is associated with higher service sector productivity (figure 3.6). Still, gains are concentrated in the most centralized areas, some of which are likely in the MCMA.

Finally, economic density can be beneficial for enhancing efficiency and productivity, but understanding the links between the two requires careful consideration. Economic density can help to maximize the benefits of agglomeration economies. It catalyzes spillover effects, innovation, research and development, and pooling of qualified labor, especially for the high-value service sector (figure 3.6). On the other hand, cities with lower economic density could also have high economic efficiency as long as people, jobs, and knowledge are well connected through good transportation networks and information and communications technology. Similarly, economic density may not be particularly relevant for manufacturing sector productivity because most of the manufacturing sector growth and productivity are driven by cost and quality of factors of production such as land, labor, and capital. In fact, the relationship between density and manufacturing productivity in Mexico shows a negative correlation, meaning the lower the density the more productive the manufacturing sector is in Mexico (figure 3.6). All of this suggests that there is no optimal level of density for economic productivity.

Infrastructure Provision and Metropolitan Coordination to Spur Economic Performance

Urbanization patterns favoring peri-urban expansion can also affect productivity by generating high costs of infrastructure. The current model of urban expansion strains infrastructure and municipal ability to maintain and expand competitive service networks. The high costs of providing infrastructure for sprawling growth limits municipal resources; these costs are passed on to firms through fees and taxes and reduce municipal capacity to encourage economic productivity outside of the construction sector. The quartile of municipalities with the lowest population density in 2010 had nearly 1.5 times more per-capita municipal spending on public works and infrastructure (table 3.2).

High savings under the counterfactual development pattern underscore the costs of the status quo. Under a more condensed urban growth scenario projected by the Secretariat of Social Development (*Secretariat de Desarrollo Social,* SEDESOL) for Los Cabos, the amount needed to build more infrastructure (roads, water provision, drainage, and electricity) could be reduced by 67 percent, from a current average of Mex$219,433 million to Mex$72,245 million. Maintenance costs could be similarly reduced, from Mex$6,134 million to Mex$1,986 million (SEDESOL 2012, and see figure 3.7). Another study for the Merida Metropolitan Area (CMM 2014) shows that the public costs for providing services infrastructure (water, sanitation, and electricity) and construction and maintenance of roads would be over 40 percent lower if the city grows in a more compact way (Mex$597 million) as opposed to a business-as-usual growth (Mex$941 million, and see figure 3.8).

In addition, economic potential and possible synergies are left untapped because of a lack of coordination at the metropolitan and regional level. A recent OECD study (2015a) found that a city's governance is reflected in its level of productivity. Cities with greater administrative fragmentation and insufficient intermunicipal coordination tend to have lower levels of productivity and have experienced lower economic growth. A metropolitan area of any given size with twice the number of municipalities is associated with about 6 percent lower productivity rates, but the existence of an effective governance mechanism at the metropolitan level can cut this effect by almost half (OECD 2015a). In Mexican

Table 3.2 Public Works Spending per Capita and Growth for Municipalities in Metropolitan Zones

Municipal density quartiles	Average per-capita spending on municipal works 2010 (Mex$)	Percentage increase in public works spending 2000–10, weighted by population growth
Highest-density	547	4.50
Medium-density	776	4.80
Lowest-density	816	3.60

Source: World Bank calculations using population data from Census 2000 and 2010; SCHP 2015.

Figure 3.7 Comparison of Cost for Infrastructure Provision and Maintenance for Different Projected Urban Expansion Scenarios for Los Cabos

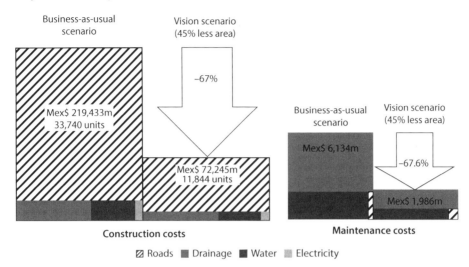

Construction costs   Maintenance costs

☒ Roads ■ Drainage ■ Water ▦ Electricity

Source: World Bank illustration based on SEDESOL 2012.

Figure 3.8 Comparison of Infrastructure Costs for Different Projected Urban Expansion Scenarios for Merida

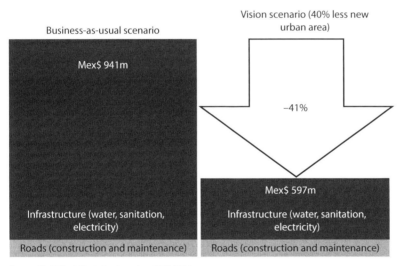

Source: World Bank illustration based on CMM 2014.

metropolises, coordination among municipal administrations is still incipient and contradictory decisions regarding infrastructure development may occur in neighboring municipal governments. Box 3.3 provides an overview of existing efforts to improve coordination and governance at the metropolitan level in Mexico.

Coordination at the metropolitan level can help to effectively manage urban growth and contribute to boosting economic growth and productivity.

Box 3.3 Metropolitan Coordination and Governance in Mexico

Although large urban areas have undertaken some attempts at coordinating metropolitan planning since the mid-1970s, comprehensive national efforts regarding designation and coordination of metropolitan areas began in earnest over the last decade. In the early 2000s, SEDESOL, INEGI (the National Institute of Statistics and Geography [*Instituto Nacional de Estadística y Geografía*]), and CONAPO (the National Population Council [*Consejo Nacional de Población*]) finalized a methodology for mapping and designating metropolitan areas (*zonas metropolitanas*). There are currently no requirements or planning obligations implied by being part of a designated metropolitan area.

The primary metropolitan-level policy instrument is the Metropolitan Fund (*Fondo Metropolitano*), a line of federal resources established in 2006 that flows through state governments to fund metropolitan projects. The Fund dispenses a significant amount of infrastructure spending for urban areas; in its first three years, it distributed over Mex$14 billion to the largest 16 metropolitan areas (SCHP 2010). By 2012, 47 officially recognized metropolitan areas received ongoing transfers through the program. The formal designation as a metropolitan area is necessary for municipalities to receive allocations or benefit from projects sponsored by the Fund.

As in other coordination mechanisms with municipalities, the process of deciding and overseeing projects financed by the Metropolitan Fund varies by state. In some states, such as Jalisco, the resources are adjudicated directly to municipalities based on a population formula with minimal oversight. In others, such as Oaxaca, a committee of representatives from various state entities reviews proposals from municipalities and grants according to their contribution to the metropolitan interest. In nearly all of the large areas, an official advisory board (*Consejo Metropolitano*) was established to bring in a wider range of state-level actors to the process. These advisory boards have no legal requirement to involve municipalities or land use initiatives in the allocation decisions.

Although metropolitan spatial planning continues to be officially represented in many state governments, for the last decade, it has lacked legal muscle as municipalities gained jurisdiction over all land use. In a handful of urban areas, such as Guadalajara, opt-in metropolitan planning centers (often called planning institutes) gather municipal councils to commit to binding resolutions for fund allocation and coordinate their spatial planning. In others, metropolitan planning efforts are being led from municipal offices, such as in Tijuana.[a] See table B3.3.1 for an overview of existing metropolitan coordination mechanisms in Mexico. Although municipal commitments are important, spatial development plans need to be linked to funding instruments such as the Metropolitan Fund to achieve their implementation.

box continues next page

Box 3.3 Metropolitan Coordination and Governance in Mexico *(continued)*

Table B3.3.1 Metropolitan Coordination Mechanisms in Mexico

Metropolitan area	*Fondo Metropolitano*[a]	*Consejo de desarrollo urbano metropolitano*[b]	*Metropolitan spatial planning entity with municipal commitments*[c]
Valle de México (Mexico City)	Y	Y	N
Guadalajara	Y	N	Y; 60% of ZM municipalities signatories
Monterrey	Y	Y	N
Puebla-Tlaxcala	Y	Y	N
Toluca	Y	N	N
Tijuana	Y	Y	N
Leon	Y	Y	N
Juarez	Y	N	N
La Laguna	Y	Y	N
Queretaro	Y	Y	Y; 100% of the ZM municipalities signatories
San Luis Potosí	Y	N	N

Note: N = no; Y = yes; ZM = *zonas metropolitanas.*
a. SCHP 2015.
b. As officially recognized and filed nationally.
http://www3.diputados.gob.mx/camara/001_diputados/010_comisioneslxi/001_ordinarias/009_desarrollo
_metropolitano/035_sedesol/003_instalacion_de_consejos_metropolitanos.
c. Including specifically metropolitan-scale entities with agreements and dues from municipalities. Notably, many urban areas
have recent metropolitan planning initiatives that are led out of the core municipality, such as Tijuana and Puebla and
Queretaro. The core municipality of Toluca recently established a citizen council for metropolitan planning, although it
appears to be primarily consultative and expert-based. In others, the state government(s) are leading a metropolitan
planning effort, such as in the Valle de México.

a. http://pem2034.herobo.com/objetivos-y-alcances-del-plan-pem2034.php.

Figure 3.9 Different Levels of Labor Productivity and Productivity Growth in Monterrey and Oaxaca, 1990–2010

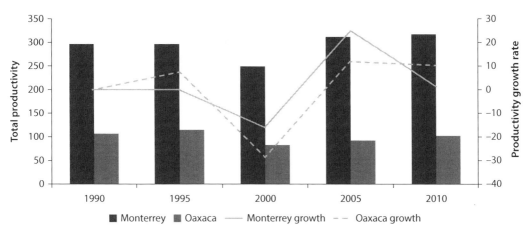

Source: World Bank analysis based on economic census data from the National Institute of Statistics and Geography *(Instituto Nacional de Estadística y Geografía,* INEGI).

Although the diversity of Mexican cities is an unquestionable asset, many analyses of Mexico's economy focus on a divergence between north and south, or formal and informal sectors. The frequently discussed factors of firms, capital, and access to borders are not trivial. However, this study suggests that differences in urban development patterns, coordination across the metropolitan area, and regional connectivity also contribute to the productivity differential. The examples of the metropolitan areas of Monterrey and Oaxaca illustrate how the growth of a classic "leader" city (Monterrey) and the challenges of a "lagging" city (Oaxaca) are deeply rooted in the characteristics of their urban expansion and the mechanisms of metropolitan governance that can help to capitalize on contiguous municipalities and regional economics (figure 3.9; boxes 3.4 and 3.5).

Box 3.4 Enforcing Cycles of Productivity Growth and Metropolitan Coordination in Monterrey

Monterrey has enjoyed decades of leadership as an industrial and manufacturing hub, anchoring many of Mexico's largest non-oil exports. Over recent years, the city has weathered an upswing in violence to become also an attractive destination for regional and international business as well as high value-added manufacturing and service activities, increasing across nearly all subsectors (figure B3.4.1).

Figure B3.4.1 High Value-Added Manufacturing and Expansion in Monterrey, 2000 and 2010

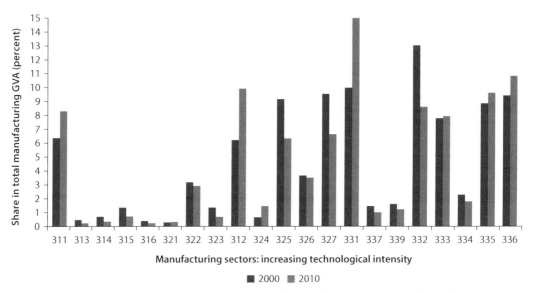

Manufacturing sectors: increasing technological intensity

■ 2000   ■ 2010

Source: World Bank analysis based on economic census data from the National Institute of Statistics and Geography (*Instituto Nacional de Estadística y Geografía*, INEGI).
Note: The numbers on the x axis are the codes for the different manufacturing sectors. A higher number in manufacturing sectors indicates a higher technological intensity. GVA = gross value added.

box continues next page

Box 3.4 Enforcing Cycles of Productivity Growth and Metropolitan Coordination in Monterrey
(continued)

By all metrics, Monterrey is leading: in 2007, the city was ranked third in Latin America by McKinsey in terms of quality of life—and best in Mexico. Monterrey's productivity growth over time is consistently near the top of the nation, and between 2001 and 2011, the city outpaced national GDP growth by 140 percent, which was also the highest percentage across Latin American cities (Mercer 2015). Further, the city is ranked third among Mexican cities for ease of starting a new business, according to the World Bank (2014).

Monterrey's strong framework and progress in urban infrastructure and amenities have facilitated this leadership. While there is always space for improvement, coalitions across agencies and municipalities frequently occur to facilitate efforts for the metropolitan interest. Within days after Hurricane Irene hit the city in 2009, a cross-entity group was formed that facilitated a speedy and coordinated rebuilding and recovery process. Similarly, institutions and working groups have developed to facilitate long-term investments. The city's water and sanitation authority, *Servicios de Agua y Drenaje de Monterrey*, operates at the state level, and has been recognized as a global leader for metropolitan operating efficiency and strategy. A secure source of purified water and reliable drainage, in turn, has helped shore up the core bottling and beverage industries, as well as attract new investments and global human capital.

Although Monterrey's trade connections to nearby cities and the border are well known, the city has also leveraged its regional networks and "system of cities" to secure basic services for future growth and climate resilience. For example, since a severe water shortage in the 1980s, Monterrey has assertively pursued regional agreements for water management. The most recent project in a sequence, Monterrey VI, will bring water from the Panuco River in the state of Veracruz to the Cerro Prieto aqueduct in Nuevo Leon.

Box 3.5 Stagnancy and Isolation in Oaxaca: Not Just Human Capital, but Connectivity and Missing Coordination

As a counterexample, the southern region, in particular Oaxaca, illustrates how the processes of regional contagion and clustering can also function to slow productivity growth. Oaxaca is often used to illustrate the failings of productivity in southern cities, where populations continue to grow and the states continue to urbanize, but economic densities are slow to rise. Oaxaca, in particular, remains reliant for most of its growth on a single industry, tourism, which has proved volatile to shifts in the national and international economic capacities and tastes, and is still recovering from downturns due to the urban unrest of the mid-2000s.

Although the state receives more federal transfers per capita than almost anywhere else in Mexico, planning constraints are holding Oaxaca back from unlocking private growth. Land use and infrastructure are haphazard, and nearly all of new urban growth has occurred in

box continues next page

Box 3.5 Stagnancy and Isolation in Oaxaca: Not Just Human Capital, but Connectivity and Missing Coordination *(continued)*

peripheral towns with little ability to service developments or provide transport or transit links to the urban core.

Further, metropolitan coordination in Oaxaca has been minimal by all accounts, and state and municipal land use plans, if in existence or published, are rarely coordinated with each other. As a result, funds for infrastructure, such as the Metropolitan Fund, despite the formation of a new committee in the past several years, are typically awarded in an ad hoc and nonspatial manner without reference to long-term strategy.

Regional connectivity is also part of Oaxaca's story, but thus far the city has not been able to unlock links to allow firms to grow. Although productivity in cities such as Oaxaca faces firm-level constraints, such as low human capital, Lall et al. (2002) found that transport infrastructure to link southern cities to markets and innovating neighbors also prevents major gains in productivity growth.

Activating Metropolitan Clusters Inside Regional Networks and "Systems of Cities"

Productivity is contagious and creates clusters of high and low growth. A spatial analysis of productivity clusters, using the Local Indicators of Spatial Association method (LISA), shows that clusters of high and low productivity have emerged in Mexico over the past decades (see map 3.4).[5] Clusters are highlighted where municipal productivity is more similar to productivity in neighboring municipalities. These findings suggest that municipalities across the country were much more likely to have similar productivity rates to their neighbors in 2008 than twenty years earlier, when sharper distinctions in productivity divided adjacent areas. This trend can lift the productivity of municipalities with the right neighbors; almost all of the low-performing municipalities in the 1980s that were surrounded by high-productivity neighbors had reached at least average productivity rates by 2008, including the Chihuahua cluster, the Saltillo cluster, and the Monterrey cluster.

Despite these effects, only a few areas have managed to catalyze a virtuous cycle of high productivity. Indeed, while growth has centered in urban areas, only a handful of new productive clusters have emerged over the last two decades. The municipalities near the border of Chihuahua, Saltillo, and Monterrey are the principal municipalities to present a growing cluster in recent years, along with a string of municipalities in the Bajío region.

As much as metropolitan regions can do on their own, networks with other cities and transport links contribute to the success and resilience of urban economies. International experience suggests that the productive potential of cities across the country can be catalyzed through a framework of urban systems. Colombia's recent policy experiences suggest that significant analysis on the existing and potential economic relationships and bottlenecks on intercity

Map 3.4 Local Indicators of Spatial Association (LISA) Cluster Maps for Productivity, 1999 and 2009

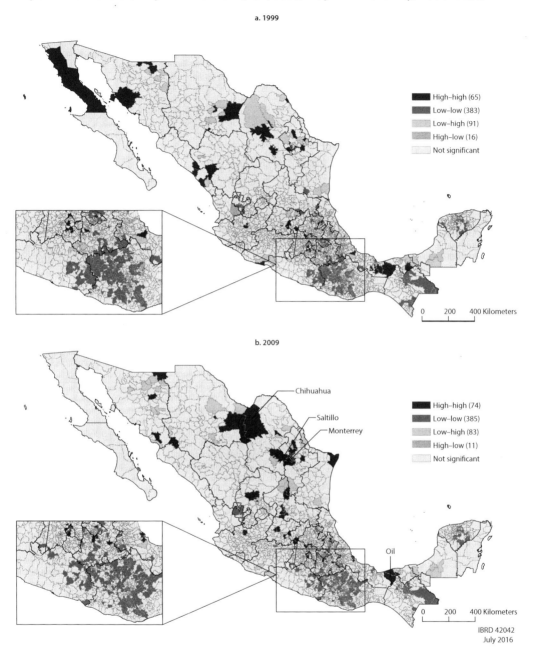

Source: World Bank analysis based on economic census data from the National Institute of Statistics and Geography *(Instituto Nacional de Estadística y Geografía,* INEGI).

synergies can be a critical component to launching a national framework based on urban systems (Samad 2012). Differentiation of policy based on the unique productive profile of cities was one major finding of advances in Colombia and other countries pursuing a system of cities approach. Instead of determining allocations based on tiers of city size or rough regions, a wide range of more sophisticated measures helps guide targeted interventions to connect and leverage urban growth and innovation. Mexico could also benefit from well-articulated and differentiated regional policy for economic development and specialization.

Given the allocation of responsibilities across levels of government,[6] the federal government's role for policy actions can be enhanced by focusing on providing the right incentives to the local and state level and playing an active coordination role. The right incentives to state and municipal governments would allow aligning the national policy objectives, such as compact and sustainable urban development, with local-level land use decisions. For instance, the federal government could work with local government to promote urban redensification by piloting a financial incentives scheme. The federal government could also take the lead in strengthening and partnering with planning institutions to strengthen planning capacity at the local level. Finally, the government could take up a more active coordination role between different levels of government as well as with different agencies working on urban issues. One immediate example would be better coordination between the urban and housing policy promoted by SEDATU (the Ministry for Rural, Territorial, and Urban Development (*Secretaria de Desarrollo Agrario, Territorial y Urbano*) and infrastructure or transport investment by BANOBRAS (National Works and Public Services Bank [*Banco Nacional de Obras y Servicios Públicos*], Mexico's state-owned development bank).

Notes

1. City center corresponds to the historic central business district, which is in most cases the city's *zócalo* and in many cities also the geographic center.

2. The density gradient of population in the 100 largest cities in Mexico ranged from less almost 0 to 0.8, with an average of 0.15, whereas the density gradient for jobs ranged from less than 0.01 to 1.2 with an average of 0.3. Higher density gradients indicate greater concentration of people or jobs.

3. The OECD study (OECD 2015a) suggests that productivity increases by 2–5 percent for a doubling of population size. This trend is attributed to several factors, including greater competition or deeper labor markets, a more diverse entrepreneurial environment and faster spread of ideas. However, in the OECD comparison, this trend cannot be observed in Mexico.

4. Monterrey, Monclova-Frontera, Coatzacoalcos, Hermosillo, San Juan del Rio, Ciudad del Carmen, Querétaro, San Luis Potosí-Soledad, and Villahermosa.

5. The cluster map shows the areas with significant local Moran statistics in different coded colors, based on the type of spatial autocorrelation. The four codes are shown in the legend: dark red for high-high, dark blue for low-low, pink for high-low, and light

blue for low-high. These four categories correspond to the four quadrants in the Moran scatter plot, where each quadrant corresponds to a different type of spatial autocorrelation: high-high and low-low for positive spatial autocorrelation—also called *spatial clusters*—and low-high and high-low for negative spatial autocorrelation—also called *spatial outliers*. Whereas spatial outliers are normally individual locations by definition, spatial clusters are normally a group of locations (Anselin 2005).

6. According to the 2014 Housing Law (*Ley de Vivienda*), the federal government is in charge of formulating and defining the national housing plan, setting the financing mechanism for housing, and promoting metropolitan programs with states and municipalities. State government is responsible for formulating state-level housing programs, supporting municipalities in planning, resource management and operation of programs on land and housing, and incentivizing the participation of social and private sectors on housing actions. Municipalities define and implement municipal programs on land and housing, define areas for housing development, implement and evaluate the state housing program, and provide public services to lands subject to housing programs from federal, state, and municipal housing plans. Road construction and maintenance are split between the three levels, with the construction mainly executed by federal and state governments, and maintenance mainly being done by the state or municipalities.

References

Anselin, L. 2005. "Spatial Statistical Modeling in a GIS Environment." In *GIS, Spatial Analysis and Modeling*, edited by D. Maguire, M. Goodchild, and M. Batty, 93–111. Redlands, CA: ESRI Press.

CABE (Commission for Architecture and the Built Environment). 2008. *Creating Successful Masterplans: A Guide for Clients*. London: CABE.

CMM (*Centro Mario Molina*). 2014. *Ciudades: Mérida Ciudades de Crecimiento*. Mexico City, Mexico: Estudios Estratégicos sobre Energía y Medio Ambiente A.C.

Garner, G. 2011. *Johannesburg: Ten Ahead: A Decade of Inner-City Regeneration*. South Africa: Double G Media.

Glaeser, Edward L. Hedi D. Kallal, José A. Scheinkman, and Andrei Shleifer. 1992. "Growth in Cities." *Journal of Political Economy* 100: 1126–52.

Government of the District of Columbia. 2010. *Anacostia Waterfront Initiative: 10 Years of Progress*. Washington, DC: Government of the District of Columbia.

Jaffe, Adam, Manuel Trajtenberg, and Rebecca Henderson. 1993. "Geographic Localization of Knowledge Spillovers as Evidenced by Patent Citations." *Quarterly Journal of Economics* 108 (3): 577–98.

Jones, Tony Lloyd. 2000. "Compact City Policies for Megacities: Core Areas and Metropolitan Regions." In *Compact Cities: Sustainable Urban Forms for Developing Countries*, edited by Mike Jenks and Rod Burgess, 46. London: Taylor & Francis.

Lall, S., U. Deichmann, M. Fay, and Jun Koo. 2002. "Economic Structure, Productivity, and Infrastructure Quality in Southern Mexico." Policy Research Working Paper 2900, World Bank, Washington, DC.

Lucas, Robert E., and Esteban Rossi-Handberg. 2002. "On the Internal Structure of Cities." *Econometrica* 70 (4): 1445–76.

Mercer. 2015. *Quality of Living Survey*. Retrieved from http://www.uk.mercer.com /newsroom/2015-quality-of-living-survey.htm.

Monkkonen, P. 2011. "Do Mexican Cities Sprawl? Housing Finance Reform and Changing Patterns of Urban Growth." *Urban Geography* 32 (3): 406–23.

———. 2014. "The Role of Housing Finance in Mexico's Vacancy Crisis." Working Paper 2014-22, UCLA Ziman Center.

OECD (Organisation for Economic Co-operation and Development). 2013. *OECD Economic Surveys: Mexico 2013*. Paris: OECD.

———. 2015a. *The Metropolitan Century, Understanding Urbanization and Its Consequences.* Paris: OECD.

———. 2015b. *OECD Urban Policy Reviews: Mexico—Transforming Urban Policy and Housing Finance*. Paris: OECD.

Samad, T. 2012. *Colombia Urbanization Review.* Washington, DC: World Bank.

SCHP (*Secretaría de Hacienda y Crédito Público*). 2010. *Evaluación del Fondo Metropolitano, 2006–2009.* Mexico City, Mexico: SCHP.

———. 2015. *Evaluación de los Fondos Metropolitano Regional del Gobierno.* Mexico City, Mexico: SCHP.

SEDESOL (*Secretariat de Desarrollo Social*). 2012. *Estudio de Implicaciones de los Modelos de Crecimiento en el Costo de Infraestructura: Caso de Estudios Los Cabos.* Mexico City, Mexico: SEDESOL.

Tiesdell, S., and D. Adams. 2011. "Real Estate Development, Urban Design and the Tools Approach to Public Policy," in *Urban Design in the Real Estate Development Process*, edited by S. Tiesdell and D. Adams. Oxford, UK: Wiley-Blackwell. doi: 10.1002 /9781444341188.ch1.

World Bank. 2014. *Doing Business in Mexico 2014.* Washington, DC: World Bank.

CHAPTER 4

Moving toward More Livable and Inclusive Mexican Cities

Introduction

The unplanned expansion of Mexican cities in recent decades has affected their ability to foster livability and social inclusion and exacerbated spatial disparities in access to services, urban amenities, and job opportunities. The spatial structure and urban design of a city contribute to shaping its livability and social inclusiveness. Livable and inclusive cities facilitate a good quality of life for all their residents. In addition to providing reliable urban services, affordable housing, and safety, livable cities also offer employment opportunities as well as adequate physical and cultural amenities, including parks, public spaces, museums, libraries, restaurants, and shopping, attracting residents and companies. Livable cities are typically also organized in a way that is conducive to connectivity and accessibility and that also addresses environmental and health concerns through the minimization of negative externalities from the urbanization process, such as congestion and pollution. Inclusive cities focus on closing the gap on the "last mile" to making housing, services, jobs, and amenities accessible for the urban poor.

This chapter analyzes the repercussions of the current spatial form of Mexican cities on their potential to foster livability and social inclusion. It will examine trends in the coverage and quality of basic services in Mexican cities. A detailed case study of the Guadalajara Metropolitan Area (GMA) will be used to illustrate how recent urban expansion has affected the lives of the urban poor in terms of access to services, amenities, and jobs; connectivity; and cost of living. It will also look at environmental and health considerations stemming from urban sprawl.

Persistent Inequality in Basic Services *within* Cities

Cities in Mexico have reached almost universal coverage of basic services. Between 1990 and 2010, access to basic services, in particular official water and sewerage services, has improved on average in cities with more than 100,000 inhabitants (see figure 4.1). A particularly positive trend can be observed for sewerage, where substantial improvements were achieved in every city size group over the past two decades. For instance, access to sewerage increased from 61 percent in medium cities and 63 percent in big cities in 1990, to over 90 percent for both in 2010. Over 90 percent of households living in cities of all sizes had access to official water provision in 2010, a significant improvement when compared to coverage levels of about 80 percent in 1990.

However, problems in quality in the provision of basic services persist. Less than 40 percent of residual waters are treated, and water companies still have serious efficiency problems regarding distribution (30 percent of water gets leaked in the water distribution network), billing system, and tariff collection (Olivares and Sandoval 2008). Where there is no systematic information

Figure 4.1 Water and Sewerage Coverage by City Size, 1990 and 2010

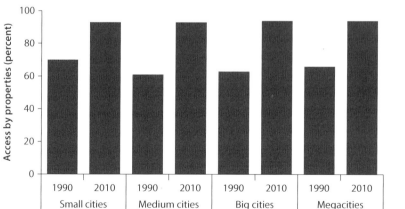

Source: World Bank analysis based on data from the National Institute of Statistics and Geography (*Instituto Nacional de Estadística y Geografía,* INEGI).

about the quality of service across different city size groups or regions, anecdotal evidence points to the need to step up the quality aspects.

In addition, coverage of public services can vary greatly *within* cities, particularly as they continue to sprawl without corresponding extension of infrastructure and service networks. Urban sprawl results in higher costs for extending service coverage to new housing developments on the outskirts of cities, making it harder for governments—particularly local governments—to finance the building and maintenance of infrastructure. As discussed briefly in chapter 3, the increasing construction and maintenance costs associated with the recent peri-urban expansion of most Mexican cities may lead to non-extension of infrastructure, or deficient provision of services. This dynamic generates striking differences in the urban landscape, leading to the coexistence within the same city of central areas that are well equipped and others that are deficiently equipped and disconnected. Map 4.1 illustrates the case of patchy service provision within the GMA; access to water, sewerage, and electricity remains very low in the urban periphery, especially in the south where most of the recent urban expansion took place, whereas central areas are well served. See box 4.1 for another example in the Metropolitan Area of Oaxaca.

Map 4.1 Infrastructure Access in the Guadalajara Metropolitan Area, 2000

Infrastructure index
Guadalajara, Mexico, 2000

■ Very high
■ High
■ Low
■ Very low
■ No data

0 1 2   4 Miles

Source: World Bank analysis based on census data from the National Institute of Statistics and Geography (*Instituto Nacional de Estadística y Geografía*, INEGI).[a]
a. The Infrastructure Index for Guadalajara was generated using the 2000 INEGI census data. The index looks at the total number of houses per census tract that lack water infrastructure, drainage, or electricity and is then normalized by the total number of inhabited houses in the census tract. These values are then summed to create the final index values. The index values were calculated by using quartiles, which were defined as the following four categories: very low (0.138–2.00), low (0.021–0.137), high (0.006–0.020), and very high (0–0.005).

Box 4.1 Urban Sprawl and Its Consequences in Oaxaca

In Oaxaca, housing developments that were built on peripheral municipalities, such as San Pablo Etla or Santa Cruz Xoxocotlán, undergo problems of water deficiency, low (or no) accessibility to public transportation, and insecurity and crime. Because of the scarcity of water—and the costs associated with extended water infrastructure—in some areas, indigenous communities and local governments refuse to provide regular access to water to new mass housing developments.

The fact that developments are placed on remote lands with great distances and empty land between them and downtown Oaxaca (or other urban centralities) make it unattractive and expensive for public transportation to serve the isolated developments. Even though there is an absence of empirical research on residents of peripheral areas' expenditures on transportation, anecdotal information highlighted the reliance on private cars and increased expenditure on gas (compared to when families lived in downtown Oaxaca).

Municipal officers expressed concern on crime rates among the youth in some of the newer developments. They claimed that youth's social, physical, and economic disconnect from the city encouraged them to engage in criminal activities. These concerns have led peripheral municipalities to refuse building permits for INFONAVIT (Federal Institute for Workers' Housing [*Instituto del Fondo Nacional de la Vivienda para los Trabajadores*]) developments.

Many existing developments located on the periphery have evolved as segregated or isolated neighborhoods, strictly designed as residential dormitories, and far away from services (for example, hospitals, schools, and amenities), jobs, and the lively dynamics of mixed-use urban spaces.

Source: Information extracted from field research and interviews conducted in the Metropolitan Area of Oaxaca in August 2014.

Uncoordinated Urban Expansion and Its Effects on Fostering Inclusive Growth and Livability

As Mexican cities have been expanding, low-income households have been moving further away from economic activities to new affordable housing developments in the urban periphery that lack adequate access to jobs, services, and urban amenities. This report carried out a case study of the GMA to analyze in more detail the socioeconomic implications of prevailing urban expansion patterns in Mexican cities that have not been well coordinated with the development of public infrastructure and services. Box 4.2 provides relevant background information on the GMA in general and its urban expansion over the past decades in particular.

In the case of the GMA, there is a north and south divide with wealthier households tending to live in the more established areas in the north and northwest, whereas lower income populations cluster in more recent developments on the city's southern and eastern fringes. Most of the recent urban expansion in the GMA happened in the southern areas and largely through the construction of lower cost, small properties. As figure 4.2 shows, properties in the south, southeast, and southwest have among the lowest median housing values in the GMA; in 2013, the southwest had the lowest appraisal value at Mex$163,000 (approximately US$11,000). In contrast, the greatest housing values are typically found in the northern and western areas of the city. In particular, the housing values in the north have appreciated every year with the exception of 2010, reaching the highest median appraisal value in the GMA of close to Mex$1 million in 2013 (approximately US$66,000). The greatest growth of housing values was observed in the west, where they appreciated 60 percent in just one year to reach a median of nearly Mex$900,000 (approximately US$60,000) in 2013. Similarly, properties in the southern side are 48 percent smaller at the median than those in the north (roughly 51 square meters compared to over 98 square meters).[1] This type of urban expansion differs from the urban sprawl

---

Box 4.2 Urban Expansion in the Guadalajara Metropolitan Area

With a population of 4.3 million and an urban area of 61,024 hectares in 2010, the Guadalajara Metropolitan Area (GMA) is the second biggest city in Mexico. It extends across eight municipalities in the State of Jalísco. Between 1990 and 2010, it experienced an average annual population growth rate of 2.2 percent, which roughly corresponds to the median of 2.3 percent for Mexico's 100 biggest cities. During the same period, its urban area grew on average 2.7 percent, which is fast compared to the median of 1.5 percent for the country's 100 biggest cities. In other words, its population increased 54 percent in 20 years, whereas its area grew by 72 percent in the same period. As a result of this growth pattern, the average population density in the GMA declined from 80 inhabitants per hectare in 1990 to 71 in 2010. However, it is still the city with the second highest average population density in Mexico.

Most of the recent urban expansion of the GMA happened on the city's southern and eastern fringes by transformation of formerly rural land into dispersed suburbs. Since 2000, most urban expansion, measured by the number of new urban census tracts every five years, is observed in the southern and eastern region[a] (in particular in the municipalities of Tlajomulco de Zúñiga, El Salto, and Tonalá), where rural land designated for agricultural purposes (*ejidos*) was urbanized. In contrast, the city's more traditional areas located in the central and northern regions (largely within the municipalities of Guadalajara, Tlaqueplaque, and Zapopan) experienced fewer changes (map B4.2.1).

This spatial expansion is largely correlated with population changes in the GMA. The central municipality of Guadalajara lost 1 percent of its population between 2000 and 2010. In contrast, the southern and southeastern areas have experienced population growth and increasing densities in the same period, in particular the municipality of Tlajomulco where population grew by nearly 13 percent. Although they have been rapidly urbanizing, the southern municipalities still remain largely agricultural, with more than 50 percent of the land in both Tlajomulco and El Salto and nearly 90 percent in Ixtlahuacán being used for agricultural purposes.

---

box continues next page

Mexico Urbanization Review • http://dx.doi.org/10.1596/978-1-4648-0916-3

Box 4.2 Urban Expansion in the Guadalajara Metropolitan Area *(continued)*

Map B4.2.1 Urban Expansion in the Guadalajara Metropolitan Area, 2000–10

Source: World Bank analysis based on data from State Population Council, State Government of Jalisco, Mexico.
Note: ZMG = Guadalajara Metropolitan Area (*Zona Metropolitana de Guadalajara*).

Although gated communities for the rich are prevalent in other metropolitan areas of Mexico, this tendency is not yet observed in the GMA, where over 80 percent of the dwellings are actually independent single-house units, followed by apartments in buildings (nearly 10 percent on average). As in other Mexican cities, the GMA has high levels of property owner-ship, whereas renting and borrowing are less important.

a. A wealth of different data sets was used for analyzing the case of the Guadalajara Metropolitan Area, including data from INEGI, CONEVAL, and SHF. While some of these data were available at Basic Geostatistical Area (*Area Geoestadística Básica*, AGEB) level, others were at the locality or postal code levels. In order to analyze these different data sets and draw conclusions that would be comparable across space, the information within the metropolitan area was aggregated by geographical location, dividing the whole urban area of the Guadalajara Metropolitan Area into nine different regions: center, north, south, east, west, northeast, northwest, southeast, and southwest. Although the geographical area is the same for all regions, the number of localities and AGEBs is not homogeneous. Refer to appendix C for a detailed description of the methodology and data used for the Guadalajara case study. CONEVAL = National Council for the Evaluation of Social Development Policy; INEGI = National Institute of Statistics and Geography; and SHF = Federal Mortgage Society.

in the United States, where higher income populations moved out of the city to the suburbs in search of larger properties (lower price per square meter). Box 4.3 provides further comparison of urban sprawl in Mexico and the United States.

Not only is the south the area where most urban expansion has been taking place, but it also concentrates informal housing with lower access to services

Figure 4.2 Median Housing Assessment Values by Geographical Location in the Guadalajara Metropolitan Area, 2008–13

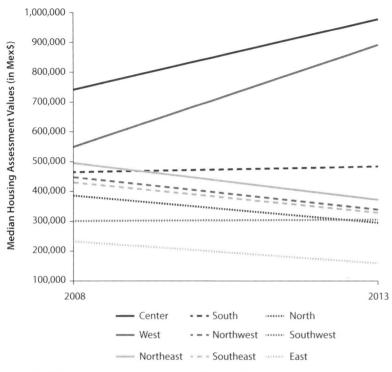

Source: World Bank analysis based on data from Federal Mortgage Society.

Box 4.3 Comparing Urban Sprawl in Mexico and the United States

There are four generally agreed upon periods of urbanization in the United States: an early urbanization period of movement from the countryside to cities (throughout the 19th century but especially after the American Civil War), a period of suburbanization when the suburban parts of cities were developed (the early 20th century), a time of counterurbanization where the urban population moved out of the city core to the suburbs (middle of the 20th century), and the present period of reurbanization in which the populations of city cores are once again growing (Champion 2001).

The suburbanization of the United States had many causes. One of the most important was the improvement of transportation technology (streetcars and automobiles, as well as freight trucks) and investment in transportation infrastructure, like the interstate highway system (Baum-Snow 2007; Mieszkowski and Mills 1993). Additionally, fiscal incentives built into the U.S. system of incorporated cities meant that the newly created suburban towns could provide better public services for lower tax rates because they were not saddled with the same debt burdens of large, older central cities (Katz 1998). Other recognized causes include rising incomes (Margo 1992), deindustrialization (Wachter and Zeuli 2014), and housing policy that

box continues next page

Box 4.3 Comparing Urban Sprawl in Mexico and the United States *(continued)*

favored lending in suburban jurisdictions, partly due to racial discrimination against communities in central cities (Jackson 1987).

   American suburbanization is characterized by low-density developments of single family
housing in the suburbs, which negatively affect the efficiency of urban form. Their low density
implies much greater per capita infrastructure costs and costs for services such as fire and
police protection; single-use residential zoning leads to wasteful commuting because retail
and other services are not spatially distributed among the population; and the increasing distance from central cities makes commute times unnecessarily long, exacerbating congestion,
pollution, and other problems associated with travel in private vehicles. Also suburbanization
is often associated with the middle class phenomenon in which households move to suburbs
looking for more space with better amenities and education facilities.

   In Mexico, urban growth was accelerated through rural–urban migration between the
1950s and 1960s, which was a consequence of the poor opportunities for workers in the countryside and the increasing labor demand in cities (Kehoe and Meza 2011). From 1960 to 1980,
the number of cities in Mexico increased from 119 to 229, and the urban population grew from
41.2 percent in 1960 to 56.2 percent in 1980 (Garza 1999). However, cities were not prepared
to receive large incoming populations, and thus this migration was accompanied by poverty
and segregation. Mexican cities developed with defined spatial differentiation between
income groups: high-income groups dominated in center cities, whereas low-income groups
were more concentrated in the periphery and urban areas not suitable for housing infrastructure or public services provision (Ingram and Carroll 1981). More recently, Mexican cities have
developed unevenly, with residential archipelagos in which residents, segregated by income
and socioeconomic status, share certain amenities in "gated communities" (Pérez Campuzano
and Santos Cerquera 2011).

   Much like in the United States, wealthier populations left the center city to access larger
properties, bigger houses, and amenities, such as pools, golf clubs, and gym facilities at affordable prices. Moreover, since the 1990s, urban sprawl in Mexico has been affected by housing
policies, based on massive funding for new housing for middle-income groups and social
housing on peripheral land, where land was less costly and farther away from the urban centers (SEDATU 2013). However, this type of peripheral development has not been necessarily
accompanied by infrastructure investment and coordination between housing financers and
municipalities.

   In Mexico, peri-urban housing developments from the last three decades differ from
traditional suburbanization in the United States in several significant ways. First, they have a
relatively high density (Monkkonen 2011). Cities expanded rapidly between 1990 and 2010.
Populations grew by a greater degree than urban areas did, leading to the increase in population densities. Additionally, the sprawl in Mexico has not been accompanied by access to
commercial activities and urban amenities; most urban sprawl in Mexico is characterized by
single-use residential areas. Nonetheless, their distance from city centers creates exactly the
same serious problems as traditional urban sprawl: dependence on private cars, congestion,
wasteful commuting times, and pollution.

and poor connectivity. Informality in housing is suggested by the fact that 86 percent of homeowners in the southwest have no tenure documents at all; accordingly, they lack access to formal credit and use their own or informal sources to finance their mortgage.[2] Despite substantial improvements in the recent past, dwellings in the southern areas seem to have poorer access to public goods and basic services as suggested by below-average values for the social lag index in the south and southeast.[3] Residents of southern neighborhoods also have lower access to urban amenities, such as schools, hospitals, parks, and rec-reational opportunities as evidenced by a median urban equipment index of one (the lowest category) in the south compared to four (the highest category) in the north in 2013.[4] Moreover, much of the recent urban developments in the south are not located close to any major road but seem to be scattered across rural areas with low connectivity. Neither are they integrated into Guadalajara's bus rapid transit system (BRT) or light rail train (LRT) (see map 4.2).

The northern area is GMA's economic hub, offering most job opportunities and attracting people from across the city with the highest wages. Nearly half of all jobs in the GMA are concentrated in the northern region, attracting not only local residents but also commuters from other regions, mostly the west, northwest, northeast, and center. Although most first commutes during the day[5] in the GMA originate and end within the same region, only the north also receives many trips from residents of other regions, mainly the neighboring northeast (42 percent)

Map 4.2 Primary Road Network and BRT/LRT Lines in the Guadalajara Metropolitan Area

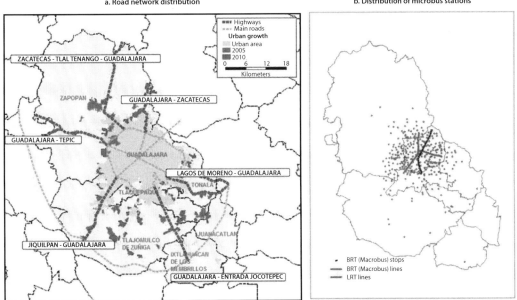

Source: World Bank elaboration based on information from SENERMEX 2012 and 2013.
Note: BRT = bus rapid transit; LRT = light rail train.

and northwest (43 percent). The average share of population working in the services sector, particularly education, in the north and northwest is more than double that in the southern areas (26.5 percent compared with 12.5 percent). The north and northwest also concentrated the highest wages in 2000,[6] whereas 13 percent of the population in the south and southwest earned only one to two minimum wages per month. In contrast, the west and the east are considered middle class regions, where 15 percent and 17 percent of the population earn between two and five minimum wages, respectively.

In the southern areas, fewer people are economically active and a higher degree of informality seems to exist in employment. While the greatest proportion of economically active population is observed in the north and northwest (46 and 45 percent, respectively), the lowest shares are found in the south (39 percent), southeast, and southwest (both 40 percent). Moreover, informality in employment seems to be high in the southwest and northeast where an alarming 71 and 66 percent of the working population did not have a job contract and 55 and 73 percent did not contribute to social security.[7] Although these findings cannot be generalized to the south and southeast, considering other aspects like housing characteristics and access to services it could be presumed that the expansion of the city on the southern and eastern side has been accompanied by socioeconomic marginalization and poorer accessibility to employment opportunities.

Effects of Spatial Growth on Commuting, the Environment, and Health

Urban dwellers in Mexico spend lengthy amounts of time commuting to work. In 2009, residents in small cities had the fastest commutes to work, spending on average 3.2 hours per week, whereas people in Mexico City spent more than twice this time (over 6.6 hours) commuting to work per week (see figure 4.3). In Mexico City, commuters using public transportation need on average 58 minutes (2009) to get from their home to their workplace; and, for those who combine public and private transportation, the trip takes over 1 hour and 21 minutes. In contrast, people who travel exclusively using private transportation need 41 minutes (IGECEM 2007). Commuting times in Mexican cities overall seem to be high when compared with the Organisation for Economic Co-operation and Development (OECD) average of just under 3.2 hours per week and the United States where citizens commute just over 2 hours each week.[8] If current urban growth trends continue and more high-density peri-urban housing developments are created without changes in the spatial distribution of economic opportunities, commuting times will likely further increase.

In the absence of accessible public transportation, coupled with increased income, the reliance on private cars increases. Between 1990 and 2013, the average number of cars per capita significantly increased across all Mexican cities with more than 100,000 inhabitants (figure 4.4). Small cities have experienced the largest increase from 0.2 cars per capita in 1990 to 0.56 in 2013.

Figure 4.3 Commuting by City Size, 2009

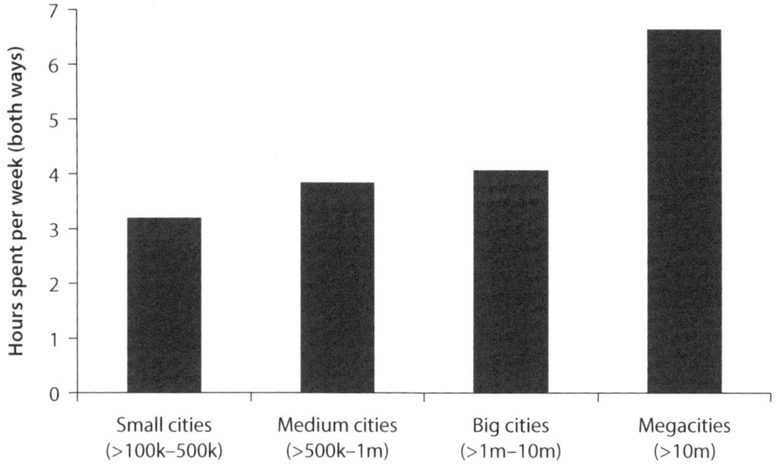

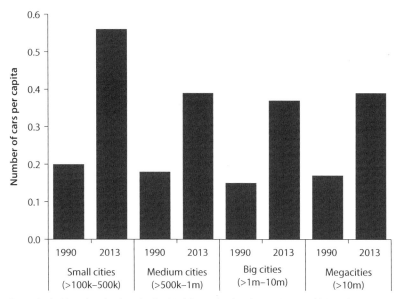

Source: World Bank analysis based on data from the 2009 National Survey on Time Use (*Encuesta Nacional sobre Uso del Tiempo*, ENUT) and the National Institute of Statistics and Geography (*Instituto Nacional de Estadística y Geografía*, INEGI).

Figure 4.4 Number of Cars per Capita by City Size, 1990 and 2013

Source: Analysis based on data from the Municipal System Database (*Sistema Municipal de Base de Datos*, SIMBAD) and the National Institute of Statistics and Geography *(Instituto Nacional de Estadística y Geografía,* INEGI).

In larger cities, this figure reaches nearly 0.4 per capita. More traffic as a result of an increased number of cars means more congestion and more air pollution within cities.

Limited access to public transportation and private cars increases the commuting burden, particularly for low-income residents living in the urban periphery. In the case of Guadalajara, the median resident of the wealthier north and center lives 4.5 kilometers and 3.2 kilometers away from the closest BRT and three LRT stations, respectively, whereas the closest stations in the south are on average about 20 kilometers away. As a result, over 32 percent of northern and central residents use public transportation for their first commute compared to only 7 percent, 17 percent, and 18 percent in the south, southwest, and southeast, respectively. Over a quarter of the southwestern population indicated that the main problem of public transport is the low frequency of trips, and 34 percent in the southeast complained about the duration and cost of trips.[9] Although new housing has been built closer to existing BRT stations since BRT's inauguration in 2009, this trend does not seem to include low-income households as evidenced by the constant minimum and maximum distances to BRT stations for the fourth quartile in 2008 and 2010 (table 4.1). Since fewer low-income households own cars, limited accessibility to public transportation affects them disproportionally and may contribute to a poverty trap.

Low-income populations living in the urban periphery also spend higher proportions of their income on transportation. On average, Mexicans spend between Mex$51 and Mex$200 daily on commuting from home to work. The percentage of properties paying this range is as much as 21 percent in cities with over one million inhabitants (SEDATU 2013). A case study for the Mexico City Metropolitan Area (CMM 2014b) found that low-income households living in peri-urban areas can spend four additional hours commuting per week and spend on average more than 15 percent of their income on transportation compared to low-income families residing in more central areas.[10] The yearly expenditures for transport of the former are more than three times higher than those of the latter (see table 4.2). A similar tendency is observed in the GMA: although the south is the region that concentrates the lower income population, individuals living in the south pay most for transportation. Over half of the southern residents paid more than Mex$100 for their first trip,[11] whereas not even one percent in the north paid this amount.

Table 4.1 Minimum and Maximum Distance to Nearest BRT Station in Guadalajara, 2008 and 2010

(meters)

	Minimum distance		Maximum distance	
	2008	*2010*	*2008*	*2010*
First quartile	198	107	8,722	7,033
Second quartile	8,738	7,131	11,870	9,581
Third quartile	11,916	9,773	18,694	18,694
Fourth quartile	18,997	18,997	32,405	32,405

Note: BRT = bus rapid transit.

Table 4.2 Comparison of Costs for the Consumer for Inner-City and Peri-Urban Housing Models

	Peri-urban cost (Mex$)	Inner-city cost (Mex$)
Land	145,496	253,260
Construction	191,828	158,748
Development	36,279	7,358
Constructor fees	17,263	15,273
Total building costs per housing unit	390,867	434,640
Annual costs of housing loan[a]	14,723	16,371
Maintenance expenses per year	2,924	2,070
Transportation costs to commute to work per year	18,216	5,819
Total yearly costs (including transport)	36,140	24,959

Source: CMM 2014b.
a. Assuming a period of 30 years and an annual interest rate of 13 percent.

In addition to shortcomings in housing infrastructure and nearby services and amenities, long commuting times and high related costs are also associated with increasing abandonment of houses in the urban periphery. Mexican housing policies over the past three decades have had positive results in terms of reducing overcrowding and housing deficit. Nonetheless, as previously discussed, uncoordinated housing developments in the peri-urban areas may also have contributed to a high level of vacant housing in Mexican cities. In the case of the GMA, higher shares of vacant housing are found primarily in the southern periphery (see map 4.3).[12] A long and expensive commute to work figures among the manifold reasons that people abandon properties, particularly people from low-income households. According to a survey of homeowners conducted by the Federal Institute for Workers' Housing (*Instituto del Fondo Nacional de la Vivienda para los Trabajadores*, INFONAVIT), the main reasons given for abandoning their urban property were the lack of service provision (38 percent) and a long commute because of the property's location (31 percent) (INFONAVIT 2012).[13]

Socioeconomic inequalities are deepened over time because peri-urban housing is more costly in the long term than inner city housing, for both the residents and the government. A study from the *Centro Mario Molina* (CMM) found that vertical social housing in more central urban areas performed better in terms of costs throughout its lifecycle compared to horizontal social housing in the urban periphery (CMM 2014b). Although there are initial savings for the latter due to lower land prices in the outskirts of cities, it already incurs higher expenses for construction and processes related to development and finishing than vertical intraurban housing. Once inhabited, annual expenses related to transportation for commuting are the main contributor for pushing up the private costs of peri-urban housing. In less than four years, living in a peri-urban house starts becoming more costly than living in the city. In addition, the cost burden for the government to provide connectivity for peri-urban housing (maintenance of roads and transport subsidies) is much higher than in the intraurban model (see tables 4.2 and 4.3).

Map 4.3 Housing Vacancy Rates in the Guadalajara Metropolitan Area, 2010

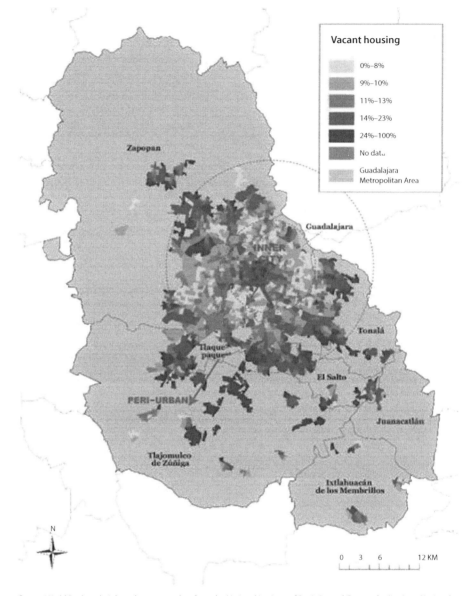

Source: World Bank analysis based on census data from the National Institute of Statistics and Geography (*Instituto Nacional de Estadística y Geografía*, INEGI).
Note: Categories in legend are quintiles.

Finally, wasteful commuting increases greenhouse gas emissions and worsens air quality in cities, creating public health challenges. According to the CMM study (2014b), the horizontal housing model in peri-urban areas generates 44 percent more carbon dioxide (CO_2) than vertical intraurban housing—mostly from transportation emissions. Similarly, another study carried out by CMM (2014a) on the implications of spatial expansion of the Mérida Metropolitan Area suggests that CO_2 emissions from public transport could be reduced by nearly one-third in an ideal growth scenario that makes full use of permitted densities in the inner city compared to the business-as-usual growth of low-density expansion. The example of the GMA also shows how air quality (measured in concentration of O_3 [ozone], NO_2 [nitrogen dioxide], SO_2 [sulfur dioxide], CO [carbon monoxide], and PM10 [particles in the air with a diameter of 10 micrometers or less]) has generally deteriorated from 2000 to 2013, despite some improvements in the city center (see map 4.4 and table 4.4).

Table 4.3 Comparison of Costs for the Government for Inner City and Peri-Urban Housing Models

	Peri-urban cost (Mex$)	Inner city cost (Mex$)
Public street lighting	4,095	2,047
Repaving of streets	20,067	4,239
Public transport subsidies	28,226	20,231
Total yearly costs for government	52,500	26,518

Source: CMM 2014b.

Map 4.4 Air Quality Index, 2000 and 2013

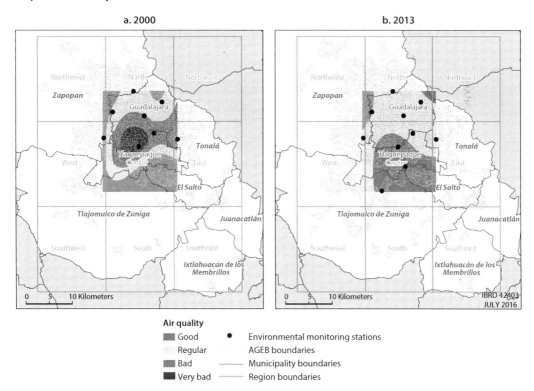

a. 2000

b. 2013

Air quality
- Good
- Regular
- Bad
- Very bad

- ● Environmental monitoring stations
- AGEB boundaries
- —— Municipality boundaries
- ---- Region boundaries

Source: World Bank illustration based on data from Air Quality Metropolitan Index (IMECA) from the Monitoring Atmospheric System of Jalisco.
Note: AGEBs = Basic Geostatistical Areas/Census Tracts (Area Geoestadística Básica).

Table 4.4 Air Quality by Region, 2000 and 2013

	No. of AGEBs with good, regular, or bad air quality, 2000				No. of AGEBs with good, regular, or bad air quality, 2013		
	Good	Regular	Bad	Very bad	Good	Regular	Bad
Center	89	86	217	96	2	220	295
Northeast	0	4	14	0	0	14	1
Northwest	7	0	0	0	9	0	0
North	41	228	53	0	18	276	3
East	6	4	20	0	0	23	11
West	12	6	0	0	4	10	0
Total	155	328	304	96	33	543	310

Source: World Bank analysis based on data from the Monitoring Atmospheric System of Jalisco.
Note: AGEB = Basic Geostatistical Area/Census Tract (*Área Geoestadística Básica*).

Notes

1. The north also has the largest properties, with three bedrooms and two bathrooms as the median, compared to two and one, respectively, in the rest of the city.

2. The Socioeconomic Conditions Module of the 2012 Income and Expenditure Survey that asks about tenure documents and source of housing finance did not include any respondents from census tracts located in the southern or southeastern regions of the city. Hence, this conclusion cannot be generalized to the whole southern side. Nonetheless, the high percentage of homeowners with no tenure documents could be seen as a proxy for housing informality in the southern side of the metropolitan area.

3. In addition to poverty measures, the National Council for the Evaluation of Social Development Policy (CONEVAL) also calculates a social lag index to assess people's nonmonetary well-being in terms of access to public goods and services. It combines weighted indicators for a range of variables, including literacy; educational attainment; access to health services; access to water, sewerage, and electricity; and certain housing features.

4. INEGI calculates an index from 1 to 4 in which each area is categorized depending on its level of urban equipment. The urban equipment is defined as those areas in which extracurricular activities are taking place, or places that offer social welfare services to the population or support to economic activities. The Federal Mortgage Society calculates a ratio surrounding the property and evaluates the urban equipment within this diameter: churches, markets, public squares, parks and gardens, schools, hospitals, and public transport stations (urban or suburban).

5. On average, 56 percent of first trips conducted by people in all of Guadalajara's regions who answered the survey were work- or school-related.

6. In 2000, 5 percent of the population living in these areas earned 10 minimum wages, whereas only 1 percent of the south and southwestern population received this type of salary.

7. Although the Socioeconomic Conditions Module of the 2012 Income and Expenditure Survey does not ask specific questions regarding informal employment, it includes questions regarding respondents' conditions at work. Two questions in particular allow us to draw some conclusions regarding employment informality: whether the

employee contributes to social security, and whether the employee has a job contract. Again, the same caveat applies that conclusions cannot be generalized because the Survey did not include any people living in census tracts located in the southern or southeastern regions of Guadalajara.

8. According to the OECD databases, the average U.S. citizen commutes 25 minutes per day, which translates to 125 minutes per work week, whereas the OECD average is about 38 minutes per day (that is, 190 minutes per work week). Mexico was not included in this database.

9. In fact, most of the answers to the specific question on the main problems regarding public transportation were obtained from people living in the northern areas. Because most public transportation is mainly located this region, households seem to be more sensitive to associated problems. On the contrary, large proportions of households in the south (55 percent), southwest (50 percent), and southeast (35 percent) did not answer the question or did not consider public transport in their answers.

10. A 2014 case study conducted by CMM examined the location of housing as a strategic aspect for sustainability and compared the carbon footprint and lifecycle costs of two types of social housing developments in the greater metropolitan area of Mexico City: horizontal peri-urban housing and vertical intraurban housing.

11. Most of the first trips conducted by people who answered the survey are work- or school-related. These two categories sum up to 56 percent on average for all regions. While the greatest percentages of individuals going to work in their first trip of the day are observed in the northeast, east, and west, the southern region shows the lowest proportion of people going to work in their first trip. For example, although this figure is 38 percent in the west, it is only 26 percent in the southwest and 31 percent in the southeast.

12. It is important to note that vacant housing does not correspond to abandoned housing, but rather vacant housing is a broader category measured by the census that includes any unoccupied property, that is, abandoned houses as well as brand new housing that has not yet been occupied, and so on.

13. It is important to note that this survey considers only properties belonging to INFONAVIT, which provides mainly affordable housing for the low-income population. The remaining reasons were: investment (10 percent), bad quality (10 percent), too small (7 percent), and insecurity reasons (3 percent).

References

Baum-Snow, N. 2007. "Did Highways Cause Suburbanization?" *The Quarterly Journal of Economics* 122 (2): 775–805.

CMM (Centro Mario Molina). 2014a. *Ciudades: Mérida Ciudades de Crecimiento.* Mexico City, Mexico: Estudios Estratégicos sobre Energía y Medio Ambiente A.C.

———. 2014b. *Vivienda Sustentable: La Localización como Factor Estratégico.* Mexico City, Mexico: Centro Mario Molina para Estudios Estratégicos sobre Energía y Medio Ambiente A.C.

Champion, T. 2001. "Urbanization, Suburbanization, Counterurbanization and Reurbanization." In *Handbook of Urban Studies,* edited by Ronan Paddison. London: SAGE Publications Ltd.

Garza, G. 1999. "Global Economy, Metropolitan Dynamics and Urban Policies in Mexico." *Cities* 16 (3): 149–70.

IGECEM (*Instituto de Información e Investigación Geográfica, Estadística y Catastral del Estado de México*). 2007. *Encuesta Origen—Destino 2007 Principales Resultados.* Mexico City, Mexico: IGECEM.

INFONAVIT (*Instituto del Fondo Nacional de la Vivienda para los Trabajadores*). 2012. *Vivienda Abandonada.* Mexico City, Mexico: INFONAVIT.

Ingram, G. K., and A. Carroll. 1981. "The Spatial Structure of Latin American Cities." *Journal of Urban Economics* 9 (2): 257–73.

Jackson, K. 1987. *Crabgrass Frontier: The Suburbanization of the United States.* Oxford: Oxford University Press.

Katz, B. 1998. *Reviving Cities; Think Metropolitan.* Washington, DC: Brookings Institution.

Kehoe, T., and F. Meza. 2011. "Catch-Up Growth Followed by Stagnation: Mexico, 1950–2010." *Latin America Journal of Economics* 48 (2): 227–68.

Margo, R. 1992. "Explaining the Postwar Suburbanization of Population in the United States: The Role of Income." *Journal of Urban Economics* 31 (3): 301–10.

Mieszkowski, P., and E. S. Mills. 1993. "The Causes of Metropolitan Suburbanization." *Journal of Economic Perspectives* 7 (3): 135–47.

Monkkonen, P. 2011. "Do Mexican Cities Sprawl? Housing Finance Reform and Changing Patterns of Urban Growth." *Urban Geography* 32 (3): 406–23.

Olivares, R., and R. Sandoval. 2008. *El Agua Potable en México.* Mexico: Asociación Nacional de Empresas de Agua y Saneamiento, A.C.

Pérez Campuzano, E., and C. Santos Cerquera. 2011. "Diferenciación Socioespacial en la Zona Metropolitana de la Ciudad de México." *Investigaciones Geográficas* (74): 92–106.

SEDATU (*Secretaria de Desarrollo Agrario, Territorial y Urbano*). 2013. *Programas Nacionales de Desarrollo Urbano 2013–2018.* Mexico City, Mexico: SEDATU.

SENERMEX *Ingeniería y Sistemas S.A. de C.V.* 2012. *Estudio de Mercado.* México.

———. 2013. *Proyecto de Transporte Masivo de Pasajeros en la Modalidad de Tren Ligero entre los Municipios de Zapopan, Guadalajara y Tlaquepaque, Jalisco.* México. (http://www.sct.gob.mx/fileadmin/DireccionesGrales/DGTFM/Proyectos _Pasajeros/Tren-Guadalajara/04_Factibilidad_Tecnica.pdf)

Wachter, S., and K. Zeuli. 2014. *Revitalizing American Cities.* Philadelphia, PA: University of Pennsylvania Press.

CHAPTER 5

Policy Messages and Recommendations

Summary of Policy Options

Using the analysis of the implications of urban spatial growth on promoting productive and livable cities in Mexico, this last chapter provides a set of policy recommendations that can help the government to better target its support for cities to improve current spatial growth and enhance productivity and livability. Table 5.1 provides a summary of these policy options, followed by a detailed policy discussion.

Reframing the Policy Lens for Productive and Inclusive Urban Growth

Housing policies have a major impact on urban form and can be tailored to encourage compact, dense, and connected growth. While the reform of housing policies in the 2000s has significantly increased the provision of affordable housing, it has also produced single-function, segregated residential developments in peri-urban areas. Government and housing authorities have recognized problems associated with this model of housing production—particularly in the face of growing abandonment rates—and new policies to create more livable spaces are being discussed, such as differentiated up-front subsidies depending on the location of housing development. Supporting social housing in planned and strategic locations within cities can help offer affordable housing for households with incomes less than five times the minimum wage, offering them alternative options to building outside the urban fringe.

Housing policies alone will not be sufficient. Urban policy and instruments should go hand in hand to manage smart urban growth and coordinate housing policies with broader urban development issues, in particular service planning and infrastructure provision, to achieve higher quality of life for all residents. Planning livable, productive, and sustainable cities is not merely about providing low-income housing or attaining high-density and

Table 5.1 Policy Options Summary

	Planning	Connecting institutions and coordination	Financing
Crosscutting: Reframing the policy lens	• Give urban policy on planning, financing, and connecting a more prominent role in guiding productive and inclusive spatial development of Mexican cities. • Underscore cities as a key driver of national economic growth and productivity. • Assess the multifaceted urban spatial dynamics and its impact in policy design. • Pivot orientation from sprawl and density to the distance and connectivity between residences, services, and jobs. • Articulate differentiated regional policies for cities' economic development to foster regional synergies across the system of cities. • Extend access to quality basic services in marginalized areas and better link lagging cities to existing markets.		
Short-term	Incentivize mixed land-use zoning for peri-urban expansion and dilapidated inner-city areas to ameliorate the negative aspects of new developments. Pilot zoning regulations to encourage the development of vibrant business subcenters.	Promote connected housing and transport-oriented developments (closer to urban centers, in infill land, using existing housing stock). Coordinate investments for infrastructure with land use planning at the metropolitan level.	Pilot innovative financing instruments with private sector participation for strategic redevelopment of inner cities and peri-urban areas to provide affordable housing and foster economic activities.
Medium-term	Encourage metropolitan-level coordination for spatial plans for expansion and subcenters. Strengthen institutional capacity of local governments for urban and land use planning by providing guidelines and setting benchmarks for performance.	Put into place concrete mechanisms for metropolitan and regional coordination to unlock economies of scale for planning and investment. Foster closer coordination among institutions responsible for housing, service provision, and planning to achieve more productive and inclusive urban growth.	Extend basic services and infrastructure, in particular transportation, at the city and metropolitan level to incorporate peri-urban neighborhoods into the urban fabric and achieve the "last miles" of universal access to high-quality services. Encourage development of well-functioning cadastral systems for Mexican cities to support financing for urban regeneration projects.

compact development. Instead, cities should facilitate a higher quality of life for their present and future residents. A significant aspect of a good quality of life is the provision of good quality basic services to all populations of a city, independent of location, income, or any other variable. High-density vertical development can be encouraged, but will not unlock the benefits of urbanization by itself. In fact, most policy instruments to influence urban growth have been led by housing policies, perhaps in the absence of strong urban policies and adequate instruments. Urban policy has an important role to play in ensuring that housing development and expected densities are tightly coordinated with available infrastructure and basic services and that networks and infrastructure systems are expanded to ensure adequate capacity for future population densities.

Current urban policy would benefit from expanding beyond density focus to incorporate multifaceted urban form into policy design. The Government of Mexico has taken several proactive measures to manage urban growth in order to promote more efficient and sustainable cities. The analysis has shown that urban spatial structure is multidimensional and complex. Although over-all Mexican cities are growing and densifying, larger cities are growing faster than smaller ones, and densities vary greatly within cities. It is important to understand the negative effects of unplanned urban expansion and shifting densities, such as household access to employment, education, and urban amenities, and excessive commuting times with their associated economic and environmental externalities. Negative consequences of current urban spatial patterns on equity are also significant, as lower income populations concentrate in the peripheral developments of Mexican cities. Although the recent policy reform is a key step in the right direction, urban policies could be further improved by broadening its focus beyond a one-size-fits-all approach to "controlling" urban expansion. It could do so by taking more measures to strengthen effective coordination and planning, and to enhance the capacity of local authorities to provide quality urban amenities and economic opportunities to all residents.

A nuanced approach to density and sprawl is needed when putting in place policy measures to influence urban growth. Higher density is considered more conducive to promoting agglomeration economies, efficient public spending, and resource allocation, but the optimal level of density varies. Similarly, uncontrolled and unconnected sprawl is not sustainable, but some level of city expansion can be efficient if the factor endowments such as land are present and if the expanded city is well connected. As an example, U.S. cities tend to be less dense than European ones but are more dynamic in terms of economic productivity and raising incomes. What is more important and relevant is to assess city-level density and spatial form, and to work on planning issues on a case-by-case approach and at a more granulated level.

Policies that frame cities as the engines of economic growth can help pinpoint the bottlenecks in the urbanization process that slow economic growth and productivity at the city or regional level. Cities are the center of production and growth for Mexico's economy. The current urban policy framework could recognize more prominently the role of cities as engines of growth and prosperity, and seek to understand the dynamics of the system of cities and how they can further contribute to economic growth.

In addition, assessing the impacts of peri-urban expansion on economic productivity can help to articulate policy measures to enhance the benefits from agglomeration economies. It is well acknowledged that high levels of informality, lack of education and skilled labor, and governance shortcomings contribute to stagnating productivity levels in Mexico. Our analysis has shown that, in addition to these factors, peri-urban sprawl brings major costs to cities and firms, and appears to have hampered improvements of productivity and efficiency by many mechanisms, including congestion, labor costs, and poor service provision. A better understanding of how urban development can support or hinder productivity gains is key to shift urban policies toward facilitating better economic growth in cities.

A national urban policy agenda could increase productivity of clusters by taking into account the tight spatial patterns or "contagion" of productivity in Mexico. Improvements in productivity have occurred in the last twenty years in a handful of adjacent municipalities. Re-orienting urban policy around an understanding of these regional and spatial characteristics can help facilitate continued growth by the leaders as well as overcome coordination, land markets, planning, and infrastructure bottlenecks faced by the lagging clusters.

The immense capacity of regional synergies across a system of cities can be best leveraged through differentiated policies. Restructuring classifications of cities around their industrial focus, sectorial function, specialization quotients, and trade links can help national entities tailor programs beyond the current metrics of city size. As a strategic national focus, it marks a major shift away from policies that focus on deficits, such as incentives for firms or people to move to lagging areas, which are often inefficient and succeed infrequently. Instead, a differentiated policy based on a finely-adapted set of productivity and innovation metrics would shift national policy to capitalize on the strengths and networks of each city within an *urban system*.

Policy makers can address persistent disparities in living standards by extending quality basic services and better linking lagging cities to existing markets. Disparities in living standards remain between leading and lagging cities in Mexico, with the latter predominantly but not exclusively located in the south where extreme poverty and inequality continue to be comparatively high. When development is inclusive and living standards converge, the benefits from growth are shared beyond the boundaries of individual cities. However, when trying to integrate lagging and leading regions, policy makers encounter the dual challenge of balancing spatial equity concerns with economic efficiency. Differentiated policies for different regions are more likely to achieve the desired balance, in particular when the overall focus of public policy is to enhance welfare everywhere. In particular, previous World Bank studies have identified as effective those differentiated policies that (i) focus on extending access to basic services in lagging areas, with the overall objective of achieving universal access and high quality of services and (ii) aim to improve market access for firms and people in lagging areas through improvements in connective infrastructure. Both types of policies can enhance the efficiency of cities while also leading to improvements in equity. International experiences also suggest that interregional transfers can drive convergence in living standards; however, they typically fail to influence economic activity, and scarce public resources may be wasted. To maximize impacts of such policies, transfers should prioritize low-income or fast-growing areas, reward areas with higher return to investment with more allocations, and ensure equitable distribution based on needs (World Bank 2009).

Planning for Productive and Livable Mexican Cities

Supporting Strategies and Instruments for Urban Revitalization

Mixed land use zoning for peri-urban expansion is an immediate action that could help ameliorate the negative aspects of new developments. As evidenced in Mexican cities, developments on the urban periphery often cause burdens both to local authorities—through the costs of incorporating amenities, infrastructure, and facilities—and to local residents, who now have to spend more time and resources to get access to the city as a place for daily social and economic exchanges. Besides promoting compact urban development, policies can encourage mixed land use as a means to reduce home-to-work commuting trips and traffic-related environmental problems. If residential and housing areas concentrate in the periphery of cities, then a more effective approach to planning would be to decentralize jobs and amenities, so as to create other urban centralities that can also offer jobs, schools, commercial activities, and other amenities at shorter distances than the traditional center.

A metropolitan approach to policies, such as metro-level plans for expansion or subcenters, can help balance jobs and housing. There is a role for public policy in addressing market failures associated with the creation of alternate employment subcenters, given the limited incentives that exist for private firms to relocate away from the central business district, even after the benefits of agglomeration economies in these districts are outweighed by negative externalities such as congestion and overcrowding. Large metropolitan areas or conurbations can plan for the development of small satellite subcenters, within and outside the peripheral areas, which can serve as growth centers for the "overspill" of jobs and residents from the central city (Jenks and Burgess 2000). This policy can be realized only if the government is able to attract private investment (for example, public-private partnerships) needed for the construction of district centers, and coordinate governance, investment, and service provision among municipalities. This approach would also require strengthened federal, state, and local efforts to identify appropriate locations for development to occur, to invest in the infrastructure needed for these developments at the metropolitan level, to enhance legal and regulatory regimes to deter irregular settlements, and to create the financial incentives for homebuyers and developers to support more sustainable housing. Moreover, spatial development policies at the metropolitan scale can be an effective mechanism to contain urban sprawl.

Close coordination with infrastructure, transport, and service planning is especially key to help recent peri-urban developments to flourish into vibrant subcenters. Even though new housing developments in Mexico continue to be predominantly horizontal, this study found that population densities in the periphery of Mexican cities are relatively high, but residents live far away from employment opportunities and often lack adequate access to public transportation and other urban services and amenities. It is crucial to better equip these areas with urban services and connect them to dynamic urban subcenters in order to draw a mix of populations and activities and help reduce the recreation of spaces segregated by income. Increasing population densities also have the advantage of reducing the unit costs of infrastructure and services. Well-organized density also brings about environmental benefits and can help save resources for services such as piped water, sanitation, garbage collection, and solid waste.

Prioritizing other high-impact and underdeveloped service expansion to the periphery, such as transportation, can also help shorten the distance to jobs. Urban connectivity is among the most underdeveloped services left behind from the process of urban sprawl. As cities continue to grow toward and beyond the urban periphery, residents' commuting distances to jobs and schools become longer. Families increasingly rely on private cars, spending more on gasoline or other forms of informal transportation services such as shared taxis or expensive privately operated minibuses or shuttles, while also contributing to increased pollution. For low-income populations who reside far from urban centers, jobs, and schools, limited connectivity and lack of transportation can severely affect quality of life and human development. It is vital that federal, local, and housing institutions discuss housing policies and programs alongside connectivity and access to mass and rapid transportation services in order to reduce segregation, inequality, and pollution, and boost productivity in Mexican cities.

Enhancing the Urban Planning Capacity of Local Governments

Efforts toward efficient and inclusive spatial growth can be sustained only if they are accompanied by strengthening institutional capacity of local governments for urban planning. Besides implementing policies that encourage compactness, high density, and service provision, efforts to improve the capacities of local governments are essential. Any benefits from high population densities can be lost by low institutional capacities to deliver services effectively and to allocate or attract necessary investment. Currently, at the state and municipal levels, low capacity and limited resources have restricted urban and land use planning functions to the preparation of plans for specific investment projects and to the development of intricate land use regulations, without any comprehensive assessment of population growth, housing and basic service needs, land use and pricing trends, growth corridors, social issues, or the capacity to implement the plans. As a result, typically, cities do not develop a strategic vision of the future (and plan accordingly); rather, they focus on separate sector programs.

The federal government can play a role in strengthening planning capacity for local authorities. A recent survey covering the 59 metropolitan areas encompassing 367 municipalities (World Bank and CMM 2015) demonstrated limited planning capacity available at the municipal level. For instance, about one-third of the surveyed municipalities did not provide any spatial information as part of their Municipal Urban Development Plan (MUDP), and a majority of the municipalities sent the information in inadequate or obsolete formats. Of the plans surveyed, only about 13 percent had a metropolitan approach. Furthermore, about 38 percent did not specify a planning period, and 40 percent of MUDPs are valid until 2030 with no clear indication of review and update before then. The federal government can consider strengthening planning institutes to support capacity building of different localities. It can also take the lead in providing standardized land use guidelines and best practices, as well as creating benchmarks for performance and compliance with planning requirements among municipalities. In addition, the federal government can consider developing incentive programs that aim to better articulate a long-term vision for city development, and better integrate land use planning, housing development, and transport investment.

Improving institutional capacity for urban planning at the local level will require developing long-term plans and visions for cities' growth and development that go beyond political terms, as well as (state and federal) tools to enforce planning guidelines and land use plans. This issue of discrepancies in long-term planning is related to the short terms of office—typically three years[1]—leading to short-term political and municipal plans and visions and substantial turnover in municipal personnel. These three-year nonrenewable terms for municipal leaders have made it more difficult to pursue stable policy and planning frameworks for land development, infrastructure, and municipal service provision.

Connecting Institutions—Coordination to Unlock Cities' Potentials for Growth and Livability

Coordination is a cross-cutting policy priority for all institutions involved in urban and housing policies. Close coordination among housing, infrastructure, transport, and services is key to helping peri-urban developments bridge the service gap and reach a higher quality of life for all residents. Economic potentials and possible synergies of Mexican cities are left untapped because of a lack of coordination at the metropolitan and regional levels. The contrast between Monterrey (enforcing virtuous cycles of growth and metropolitan coordination) and Oaxaca (stagnation and isolation without coordination) is illustrative of this.

Strengthening tangible mechanisms for coordination at the metropolitan and regional levels can unlock economies of scale for public investment and planning. Currently, there is no real legal framework for a metropolitan government structure. The metropolitan areas are managed by the municipal governments that make up the metropolitan area. There is no clear regionwide framework for sharing responsibilities or pooling resources. In addition, vertical alignment and coordination between federal and local government needs to be strengthened in order to work toward common objectives and incentives for sustainable spatial development.

Coordinating investments for infrastructure with land planning at the metropolitan level can help unlock cities' abilities to specialize and create high value-added productive sectors. Effective interinstitutional coordination and metropolitan governance are key to achieving more efficient and sustainable urban growth. With regard to improving productivity in particular, metropolitan coordination can play a key role in improving inner-city connectivity by rationalizing the provision of transport infrastructure and options across municipal boundaries and in addressing associated diseconomies of scale, such as congestion and pollution.

Improving vertical alignment of priorities and coordination of planning efforts between federal and local governments is important to ensure more efficient and equitable urban growth. The federal government must seek to include state and municipal governments as key contributors in efforts, initiatives, and decision-making processes related to urban and housing policies and programs. Although strong federal leadership on housing and urban policies is necessary, the responsibility for developing and executing land use planning falls to municipal governments. One important way to effectively address cities' spatial structure is by having municipal governments participate in housing decisions, programs, and building processes. In their effort to make housing affordable to low-income workers, developers have also been pushed beyond the urban fringe to find available and affordable land. Development of better mechanisms in federal housing programs to support the social production of housing, and municipal participation in the planning and land allocation for such housing, would help meet the needs of low-income workers.

Financing for Well-Connected, Prosperous, and Livable Cities

Strategic redevelopment of inner cities in partnership with the private sector can help provide affordable housing and regenerate downtown areas for economic activities. Rather than limiting urban growth, focusing on redensification and regeneration of existing urban centers can contribute to making inner cities more attractive and livable. Existing policy relies heavily on the use of housing subsidies to promote dense urban areas. While housing subsidies can contribute to a more sustainable urban form, additional urban instruments are needed. For example, land-based financing instruments can pay for the provision or upgrading of urban infrastructure. Land-based financing instruments include betterment levies, developer land sales, value capture via project-related land sales, the sale of development rights, developer exactions and impact fees, and land asset management. There have been a few pilot projects led by the federal government on urban regeneration together with local authorities, but they are in a nascent stage. The government could take the lead in establishing the overall framework, piloting inner-city regeneration efforts to experiment with incentives for local governments to pursue inner-city revitalization efforts.

Invest in well-functioning cadastral systems for Mexican cities. For cities to manage inner-city regeneration programs together with the private sector, fluid land markets and systems to monitor and update market movement are crucial. In particular, land-based financing instruments allow financing of infrastructure projects by tapping into the future increase in land values resulting from investment. Hence, well-functioning cadastral systems are important conditions for the innovative financing instruments to work. Cadastral systems in Mexico are generally fragmented and delegated to municipal levels without a harmonized methodology and a standardized technology. Coupled with the lack of incentives for local government to improve their municipal revenue management, there is much room for the federal government to invest in local capacity to manage the local cadastral systems.

Extending access to basic services in marginalized urban areas and lagging regions is a critical first step in incorporating peri-urban settlements into the urban fabric and fits in the overall policy objective of achieving "last miles" of universal access and, most important, a high quality of basic services. Although cities are performing much better than rural areas on service networks and provision, they are also creating unequal spaces that coexist with one another inside the same urban areas, in particular in the areas of public transportation, solid waste collection, and education and health centers. As discussed previously, this is related to the fact that housing developments, in particular those that are targeted to low-income residents, are built away from existing networks and without coordination with local governments for future provision of infrastructure and services. Thus, families who purchase homes in developments that are distanced from urban centers and networks can secure access to a formal dwelling but may suffer from a lack of a decent living environment, with low quality—or even inaccessibility to—basic services. This lag will affect families' quality of life.

Note

1. Mayors in Mexico are elected for a three-year term and in the past could not run for an immediate second term. Recent changes in federal legislation, however, concede states the right to allow immediate re-election of mayors and state representatives, though this has not yet been implemented in many states.

References

Jenks, Mike, and Rod Burgess, eds. 2000. *Compact Cities: Sustainable Urban Forms for Developing Countries*. London: Spon Press.

World Bank. 2009. *World Development Report 2009: Reshaping Economic Geography*. Washington, DC: World Bank.

World Bank and CMM (Centro Mario Molina). 2015. *Perfil Metropolitano: Escenarios de Crecimiento y Capacidad de Carga Urbana en 59 Zonas Metropolitanas*. Mexico City, Mexico: Centro Mario Molina para Estudios Estratégicos sobre Energía y Medio Ambiente.

Glossary of Urban and Housing Sectors in Mexico

BANOBRAS *Banco Nacional de Obras y Servicios Públicos* (National Infrastructure Bank). Funds large capital projects, such as new highways, dams, and sewage treatment plants.

CONAPO *Consejo Nacional de Población* (National Population Council). Tasked with strategic demographic planning strategies that align and coordinate with national economic and social policies.

CONAVI *Comisión Nacional de Vivienda* (National Housing Commission). Federal institution formed in 2001 as part of the Social Development Secretariat (SEDESOL). CONAVI became autonomous in 2006 and was put under the newly established Secretariat for Urban, Rural, and Territorial Development (SEDATU) in 2013. Develops and coordinates the national housing plan.

CONEVAL *Consejo Nacional de Evaluación de la Política de Desarrollo Social* (National Council for the Evaluation of Social Development Policy). Independent public entity to monitor policy and develop definitions and indicators for poverty.

CORETT *Comisión para la Regularización de la Tenencia de la Tierra* (Landownership Regularization Commission). As of 2013–15, is being restructured as INSUS (see below).

FONHAPO *Fideicomiso Fondo Nacional de Habitaciones Populares* (Low-Income Housing Fund). Transferred from SEDESOL oversight to SEDATU in 2013. Is a source of federal support for housing for very low-income housing.

FOVISSSTE *Fondo de Vivienda del Instituto de Seguridad y Servicios Sociales de los Trabajadores del Estado* (Housing Fund of the Social Security and Services Institute for State Workers). Provident fund for housing for public sector workers. Equivalent to INFONAVIT and with many of the same operational policies and below-market rates for mortgages.

IMPLAN	*Instituto Municipal (o Metropolitano) de Planeación* (Municipal [or Metropolitan] Planning Institute). Decentralized public authority that operates out of many major cities, and in Jalisco, at the metropolitan level, with the objective of coordinating spatial planning.
INEGI	*Instituto Nacional de Estadística y Geografía* (National Agency of Statistics and Geography). Conducts decennial census and other population and economic surveys.
INFONAVIT	*Instituto del Fondo Nacional de la Vivienda para los Trabajadores* (National Housing Fund for Private Sector Workers). Housing provident entity serving employees of formal private-sector businesses, funded by a compulsory contribution of 5 percent of salaries. Currently funds approximately 80 percent of mortgages in Mexico. Public decentralized entity, governed by representatives of workers, employers, and the government.
INSUS	*Instituto Nacional del Suelo Sustenable* (National Institute of Land Sustainability). Federal agency being created to replace the Land Regularization Commission, CORETT. As of 2014, the mission included creation of land banks, facilitating land supply for housing, regularization through a subentity assuming former tasks of CORETT, and facilitating improved information systems for land.
RUV	*Registro Unico de Vivienda* (National Housing Registry). Information platform for all new housing developments. Financed by a trust, and managed by a consulting board from the major housing and urban-related agencies. Also serves to screen applications for CONAVI's *Esta es Tu Casa* program, and calculates the location-based point and eligibility of prospective developments.
SEDATU	*Secretaria de Desarrollo Agrario, Territorial y Urbano* (Secretariat for Rural, Territorial, and Urban Development). Formed in 2013 with the mission of developing a unified national urban, housing, and agrarian policy in coordination across all levels of government. In charge of developing the National Housing Program and national Program for Urban Development, and is tasked with coordinating land, finance, and construction for new development. Several other entities and secretaries now are officially inside of SEDATU, including CONAVI, CORETT, and FONHAPO, as well as several other agrarian and land-development entities and sections of SEDESOL.
SEDESOL	*Secretaria de Desarrollo Social* (Social Development Secretariat). Federal ministry that used to be responsible for, among other things, urban development before SEDATU was

created in early 2013. Core mission is to administer social assistance programs, including the large *Oportunidades* program of conditional transfers to the poor. Involved in urban development in some areas with vulnerable residents.

SEMARNAT   *Secretaría de Medio Ambiente y Recursos Naturales* (Secretariat of Environment and Natural Resources). Manages and regulates pollution, industrial waste from large producers. Major new developments are typically required to acquire approval from the state delegate, after undergoing a review for major environmental issues for housing location (for example, in high-risk or protected areas).

SHF   *Sociedad Hipotecaria Federal* (Federal Mortgage Corporation). Decentralized public entity established in 2002 to coordinate housing finance and lead the development of primary and secondary market-rate home lending. Currently serves as a second-tier institution that provides liquidity and guarantees to first-tier lenders, with a few new programs to support housing improvement and self-construction lenders.

SOFOLES   *Sociedades Financieras de Objeto Limitado* (Mexican Special-Purpose Financial Companies). Nonbank financial institutions established to deliver housing finance to middle-income households unserved by the provident funds. Many were hard-hit in the financial crisis and now only account for a small fraction of housing lending.

SUN   *Sistema Urbana Nacional* (National Urban System). Recent initiative to classify and assemble indicators about cities, based out of SEDATU.

APPENDIX B

Methodology for Analyzing Urban Spatial Structure

Scope and Data of Analysis

We analyze the urban spatial structure of the 100 largest cities in Mexico, including all those with a population of more than 100,000 inhabitants. We calculate a number of standard measures of urban spatial structure using data from the Mexican census bureau National Institute of Statistics and Geography (*Instituto Nacional de Estadística y Geografía*, INEGI). The primary geographic data source is the *Cartografía Geoestadística Urbana* created by INEGI, which is combined with data from the population and economic censuses. The *Cartografía* is the map of all urbanized land in Mexico, created by INEGI to assist its census enumeration. Urbanized land is divided into Basic Geostatistical Areas (*Areas Geoestadísticas Basicas*, AGEBs), which are the equivalent of census tracts in other countries. They roughly correspond to neighborhoods, containing an average of 1,900 residents and covering 40 hectares.

Mexico differs from other countries in the method INEGI uses to delineate census tracts; AGEBs are defined only for urban and rural areas in separate maps. One advantage of the Mexican system is that the urban census tracts are defined only for urbanized land (with some exceptions). This means that the area of urban census tracts matches, to a large extent, a city's urbanized area and can be used in lieu of estimates of built-up areas based on satellite imagery. The urban area estimated using the area of census tracts will generally be larger than an estimate using satellite imagery. This is because in many cases census tracts in the peri-urban part of the city are drawn to include some land that is not built on. This biases population density estimates downward. Nonetheless, the overall equivalency between urbanized areas and urban census tracts has been corroborated using satellite imagery (Monkkonen 2008).

Our analysis of urban densities and spatial structure using census tracts does consider the fact that some AGEB boundaries were changed between 2000 and 2010. In general, the calculations of urban expansion over time using census tract areas will not be as precise as calculations based on satellite imagery.

Changes in the amount of undeveloped land in peri-urban tracts can skew the numbers. Fortunately, there does not seem to be a systematic bias in the data; that is, numbers are not skewed to a greater degree in larger cities or in certain regions of the country. Additionally, we do correct for the most evident errors in the AGEB data. Some AGEB boundaries are redrawn between census years to more closely follow actual urbanized land patterns. We have gone through the data to identify these cases and correct their land areas in the earlier years.

The advantage of INEGI's method of drawing census tracts is that the land area defined in the urban cartography can be used for measures of urban growth and the calculation of population density. We take advantage of this fact in the analysis presented here by using the land area and population densities calculated based on that land area to assess urbanization trends and patterns. Additionally, we rely on the information about within-city, or intraurban, variation in density patterns to calculate various measures of urban form. It should be noted that INEGI also divides rural land into rural AGEBs. The dissemination of maps and data for rural AGEBs differs substantially from the urban cartography and therefore is not included in the present study.

The *Cartografía Geoestadística Urbana* is available from INEGI for the years 2000 and 2010 in a format usable in common spatial analysis packages. Maps for year 1990 census tracts are not readily available. Therefore, for the purposes of this study, 1990 maps were created using year 2000 maps and a crosswalk table published by INEGI that lists AGEBs that were newly created between census years and AGEBs that were split into two or more new AGEBs during the interim years. We recreate 1990 maps by eliminating tracts from year 2000 maps and merging those tracts that were split. These three time periods of map enable us to calculate urban growth rates, population densities, and other indicators of urban spatial structure.

Data for the analysis come from the Census of Population and Housing of 1990, 2000, and 2010 and the Economic Census of 1989, 1999, and 2009 and are matched to the map files. Before creating metrics of urban spatial structure, we first defined city centers for each of the 384 cities in the National Urban System (*Sistema Urbano Nacional*, SUN) in order to estimate monocentricity and urban compactness. Centers correspond to historic central business districts, the city's zocalo in most cases, which in many cities are also geographic centers.

Trends in Overall Population Densities in Mexican Cities

This report finds that overall population densities in the largest 100 cities slightly increased between 1990 and 2010. Of the 100 largest cities in 2010, the median percent increase in land area between 1990 and 2010 was 34 percent, while the median percent increase in urban population was 57 percent. In other words, urban populations have grown faster than the land area of cities, making urban density go up. The increase in urban population was higher in medium and larger cities with more than 500,000 inhabitants in 2010, but on average

Table B.1 Average Population Densities from 1990 to 2010 by City Size and Region

Category	Year	Average, in persons/ hectare	Standard deviation	Change 1990–2010, in %
Mega city (Mexico City)	1990	80	—	
	2010	85	—	6.3
Big cities	1990	49.1	18.7	
	2010	49.8	12.3	1.4
Medium cities	1990	40.5	12.9	
	2010	44.8	11.3	10.6
Small cities	1990	33.9	10.3	
	2010	38.8	10.7	14.5
Border	1990	33.0	9.3	
	2010	36.6	9	11.2
North	1990	43.3	11.7	
	2010	48.1	12.2	11
Center	1990	38.3	14.8	
	2010	42.3	12.8	10.5
South	1990	34.4	10.8	
	2010	40.11	8.4	16.8

Source: World Bank analysis based on population census data from the National Institute of Statistics and Geography (*Instituto Nacional de Estadística y Geografía*, INEGI).
Note: Large cities have over 1 million and up to 10 million inhabitants, medium-size cities between 500,000 and 1 million, and small cities between 100,000 and 500,000; — = not available.

population densities increased more in small- and medium-size cities with between 100,000 and 1 million inhabitants in 2010. The number of cities with a population density over 50 people per hectare increased from 13 in 1990 to 22 in 2010. Table B.1 reports population densities for the largest 100 cities in Mexico in 1990 and 2010 by city size and region. It is important to distinguish the urbanized area from the administrative area of a municipality. The administrative area of a municipality is generally larger than the urbanized area and might contain large numbers of rural residents. Map B.1 illustrates the territorial difference between the municipality and the urbanized area for the case of Aguascalientes in 2010 (based on urban census areas from INEGI). This report used data at the level of urban locality or urban census tract to include the number of people living in the urbanized area of the municipality.

Differences in the Methodology to Calculate Population Density

The reason the 2012 Secretariat of Social Development (*Secretariat de Desarrollo Social*, SEDESOL) report calculated differently the rate of population increase compared to urban expansion is that they used population numbers for the *entire* municipality and compared them to urban land area. Using municipal population numbers to calculate urban population densities inflates densities. The dramatic drop in population densities reported by SEDESOL is the result of a decrease in the rural population of municipalities, not a decline in urban population densities.

Map B.1 The Municipality and Urban Area of Aguascalientes

San José de Gracia

San Francisco de los Romo

Jesús María

Aguascalientes

El Llano

Aguascalientes

Aguascalientes

▨ AGEBs-urban

⎯ Municipality boundaries

⎯ State boundaries

Villa Hidalgo

Encarnación de Díaz

0   5   10 Kilometers

Jalisco

IBRD 42404
JULY 2016

Source: World Bank diagram based on data from the National Institute of Statistics and Geography (*Instituto Nacional de Estadística y Geografía,* INEGI).
Note: AGEB = Basic Geostatistical Area/Census Tract (*Área Geoestadística Básica*).

Because the report uses municipal population numbers to calculate urban population densities, it includes rural residents in the numerator of the density calculation.

In addition, the SEDESOL report does not report population density numbers for 1980, but using the numbers reported for urbanized area and population yields lower densities. For instance, the report suggests that Aguascalientes went from a population density of 226 people per hectare in 1980 to 94 in 2000 and Toluca from 434 to 51. It is improbable that Toluca had a population density of 434 in 1980, which would be similar to that of Dhaka, Bangladesh. Other cities, like Tijuana, appear to have experienced very little change in population density from 1980 to 2010. What possible explanation is there for Mexicali to have decreased in density threefold while Tijuana changed little? The reason stems from the use of municipal population numbers that include rural inhabitants. Tijuana did not have a significant rural population in 1980, and thus the size of the municipal population was close to that of the urban area.

Comparing population densities from the SEDESOL report and those calculated with census data shows different results. Table B.2 reports the population and population density of the 20 largest cities in Mexico from the SEDESOL report for 1980 and 2010, and from the Census of Population

Table B.2 Urban Areas, Population, and Population Density for 20 Largest Cities

| City | SEDESOL | | | | INEGI | | | |
| | 1980 | | 2010 | | 1990 | | 2010 | |
	Population	Density	Population	Density	Population	Density	Population	Density
Mexico City	14,123	272	20,117	85	14,917	80	19,574	85
Guadalajara	2,245	176	4,435	70	2,826	80	4,323	71
Monterrey	2,062	160	4,106	52	2,617	50	4,045	53
Puebla-Tlaxcala	1,111	228	2,729	36	1,569	28	2,596	36
Toluca	568	434	1,936	38	784	34	1,537	38
Tijuana	492	81	1,751	51	750	40	1,674	50
León	733	293	1,610	66	830	84	1,438	67
Juárez	567	138	1,332	38	791	35	1,324	37
La Laguna	689	292	1,260	40	729	44	1,067	40
Querétaro	323	413	1,097	53	455	47	921	53
San Luis Potosí	471	236	1,040	53	613	49	995	53
Mérida	444	93	973	34	593	33	931	34
Mexicali	511	107	937	38	495	35	838	39
Aguascalientes	359	226	932	63	463	54	828	64
Cuernavaca	368	144	925	40	517	30	838	41
Acapulco	409	295	863	46	543	46	726	46
Tampico	437	150	859	39	574	26	786	40
Chihuahua	407	157	853	30	530	35	835	30
Morelia	353	216	830	55	452	56	707	55
Saltillo	345	230	823	34	441	22	785	34

Source: Date from the Secretary of Social Development (*Secretariat de Desarrollo Social*, SEDESOL) and the National Institute of Statistics and Geography (*Instituto Nacional de Estadística y Geografía*, INEGI).

Note: The years do not line up between the two data sources: SEDESOL reports numbers for 1980, but INEGI data only go back to 1990. SEDESOL population numbers are for municipality, INEGI's are for urban areas.

and Housing (INEGI) for 1990 and 2010. It is somewhat difficult to compare the 1980 numbers with those from 1990, but one can clearly see that the population numbers for 2010 are different. The numbers reported by SEDESOL are consistently larger than those of INEGI because they include rural residents of the municipality.

Measuring Spatial Form

There are three primary dimensions to urban spatial structure: (i) the density of population and economic activity, (ii) the relative concentration of these activities in the center versus the periphery, and (iii) the fragmentation of the city over its land area. We measure these three dimensions of sprawl using five indicators. *Density* is the simplest—the number of people or jobs per hectare. The centrality, or the concentration of people and jobs in the city center, we measure in two ways. The first is a density gradient (DG), derived from the monocentric city model, and the second is a centrality index (CI) that measures the average distance of the population relative to the size of the city (Galster et al. 2001). Urban fragmentation, or compactness, is a more complex phenomenon. We use two measures to capture different aspects of it: a proximity index (PI) that measures a city's circularity without considering the intensity of land use in different parts of the city, and a clustering index (CLI) that measures the concentration of activity and people in certain areas. Details of these five measures are presented below along with their relationship to the idea of sprawl.

1. Density. The most basic measure of urban spatial structure is density. The gross density is the number of people per hectare of urbanized land or the number of jobs per hectare of urbanized land. Of course, this overall measure ignores the great variation in density within cities, but is nonetheless useful to get a sense of the intensity of land use. Population and employment density in Mexican cities are calculated using the total urban land area measure from the *Cartografía Urbana* for each time period as the denominator. Population and job numbers come from the corresponding Census of Population and Housing and Economic Census, and have been matched to the census tract codes in the *Cartografía Urbana*.

Figure B.1 shows the variation in population densities for a sample of cities, contrasting the more sprawling Tlaxcala-Apizaco with more compact Orizaba. *Less sprawling cities have higher densities.*

2. Density gradient. Population and employment densities decline as one moves farther from the center of the city. The density gradient reflects the city's centrality by measuring the rate at which density declines at greater distances from the city center. It stems from the standard model of urban land markets and urban structure, the monocentric city model (Alonso 1964; Mills 1967; Muth 1969). This model is based on an assumption that all employment occurs in the city center, which generates a concentration of land value and population density in the center. This obviously unrealistic assumption enables the model to reflect the fundamental importance of the access of the city center as the point most proximate to everywhere else in the city. Moreover, the model yields results that are strongly upheld in reality; almost every city in the world exhibits a strong tendency toward greater density in city centers (Bertaud and Malpezzi 2003). Because density does not decrease in a linear fashion at greater distances from the city center, the gradient is best described by a negative exponential function. This takes the form: $D_s = D_0 * e^{-gs}$, where D_s is the density at distance s from the city center, D_0 is the density at the city center, and g is the gradient. Density gradients are generally negative, thus we take their inverse. *Higher values therefore indicate a steeper slope and greater monocentricity.* This is illustrated in figure B.2, focusing on the cities of Cuernavaca and Zitácuaro.

In Mexico, jobs are much more centralized than residential space. To get a visual sense of the shape of density gradients for jobs and people, figure B.3 presents gross population density at different distances from the city center for Aguascalientes, León, and Guanajuato, in 1990, 2000, and 2010; and figure B.4 shows the number of jobs in the same format. Jobs consistently have a much steeper density gradient than population does

Figure B.1 Population Density Comparison, Selected Cities with Tlaxcala-Apizaco and Orizaba

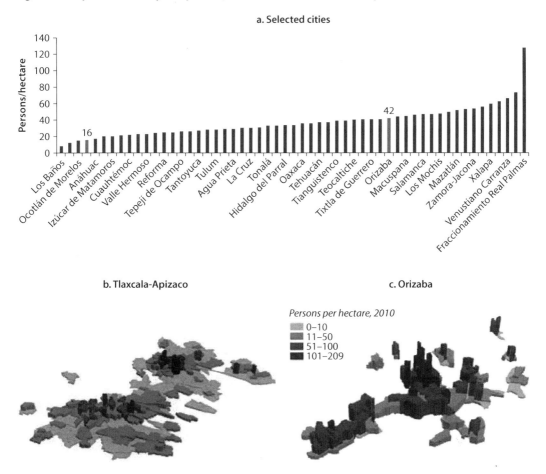

a. Selected cities

b. Tlaxcala-Apizaco

c. Orizaba

Persons per hectare, 2010
- 0–10
- 11–50
- 51–100
- 101–209

Source: World Bank analysis based on population census data from the National Institute of Statistics and Geography (*Instituto Nacional de Estadística y Geografía,* INEGI).

in Mexico. The average population density of León is higher than that of Aguascalientes, yet the population density gradient for Aguascalientes is slightly steeper—0.039 in the year 2010 compared to 0.032 in Leon—and the employment density gradient is much steeper—in Aguascalientes it is 0.14 compared to 0.06 in Leon, indicating that it has a more monocentric population and employment structure. The density gradient of population in the 100 largest cities in Mexico ranged from less than 0 to 0.8, with an average of 0.15, whereas the density gradient for jobs ranged from less than 0.01 to 1.2 with an average of 0.3. *Less sprawling cities have higher density gradient values.*

3. **Centrality index.** Density gradients measure centrality but are influenced also by the size of the city; larger cities have lower density gradients simply because of the mathematics of the calculation. Thus, we employ an additional

Figure B.2 Population Density Gradient Comparison, Selected Cities with Cuernavaca and Zitácuaro

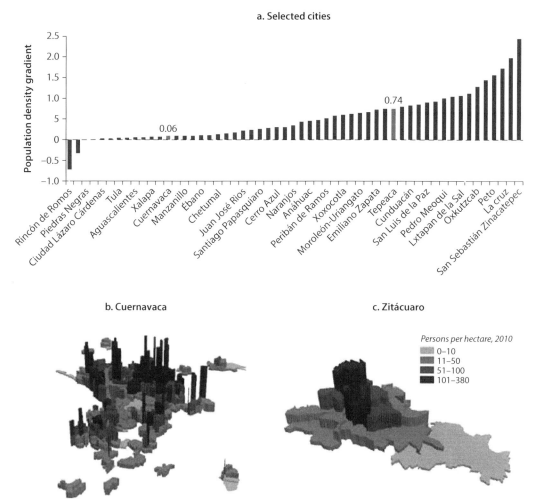

a. Selected cities

b. Cuernavaca

c. Zitácuaro

Persons per hectare, 2010
- 0–10
- 11–50
- 51–100
- 101–380

Source: World Bank analysis based on population census data from the National Institute of Statistics and Geography (*Instituto Nacional de Estadística y Geografía,* INEGI).

measure of centrality, proposed by Galster et al. (2001), to assess the average distance of the population from the center of the city, normalized by the city's area so that the measure does not simply reflect city size. To calculate this CI, we sum the inverse distance of each tract, weighted by its population. Then, we standardize this average distance by the city's size, dividing it by the square root of the total urban area. The calculation is relatively simple and yields an index with values in 2010 ranging from 0.36 to 1.95 with an average of 0.83 for population and from 0.38 to 1.78 with an average of 0.99 for jobs. This measure captures a different aspect of centrality than that of the density gradient, reflecting the combination of tract distance from the city center

Figure B.3 Population Density by Distance to City Center for Aguascalientes and Leon, 1990–2010

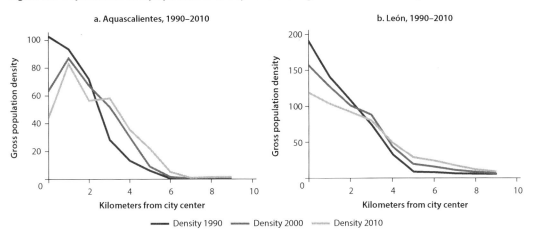

Source: World Bank analysis based on population census data from the National Institute of Statistics and Geography (*Instituto Nacional de Estadística y Geografía*, INEGI).
Note: In panel a, gradient of 0.39 in 2010. In panel b, gradient of 0.34 in 2010.

Figure B.4 Jobs by Distance to City Center for Aguascalientes and León, 2000–10

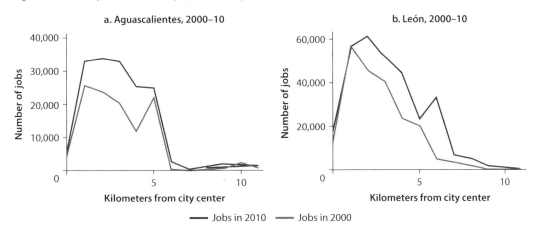

Source: World Bank analysis based on population census data from the National Institute of Statistics and Geography (*Instituto Nacional de Estadística y Geografía*, INEGI).
Note: In panel a, gradient of 0.14 in 2010. In panel b, gradient of 0.06 in 2010.

and density. As a result, Minatitlán has a lower value for the CI than Uruapan, given that more of its population lives relatively farther away from the center (figure B.5). *Less sprawling cities have higher CI values.*

4. Proximity index. The first measure of urban fragmentation or compactness assesses the extent to which a city has a circular shape, which is the most economical of urban forms. Angel, Parent, and Civco (2010) developed

Figure B.5 Centrality Index Comparison, Selected Cities with Minatitlán and Uruapan

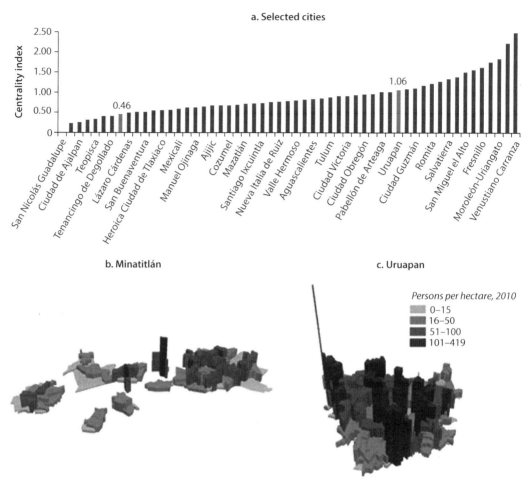

a. Selected cities

b. Minatitlán   c. Uruapan

Persons per hectare, 2010
- 0–15
- 16–50
- 51–100
- 101–419

Source: World Bank analysis based on population census data from the National Institute of Statistics and Geography (*Instituto Nacional de Estadística y Geografía,* INEGI).

the PI to assess urban compactness. This compares a city's geometric shape to that of a circle, varying from 0 to 1, where 1 indicates the city is a perfect circle and 0 is a linear city. It is calculated by creating an "equal area circle," which is a circle with the same area as the city, centered at the city center. Then, the average distance of all tracts within that circle to the city center is divided by the average distance of all tracts in the city to the city center.

We make one important improvement to the index proposed by Angel, Parent, and Civco (2010); we also factor nondevelopable land into the calculation. Nondevelopable land in this case refers to three categories of space that cannot be built upon because of natural geographic constraints (water bodies and steep slopes) or international borders (land not located in Mexico for border cities). These cannot form part of urbanized land in cities, and this should be factored into the estimation of the equal area circle. Therefore, to calculate the PI, we add the area of water bodies and steeply sloped land to the equal area circle. Map B.2 shows the equal area circles for the city of Aguascalientes and Acapulco, cities that are quite different in shape. Aguascalientes is fairly circular, thus giving it a higher PI value (0.71) than Acapulco, which is decidedly not circular, even after factoring in the water bodies and steep terrain (PI of 0.59). The average PI value for the 100 largest cities is 0.63, and it ranges from 0.14 to 0.95. Figure B.6 compares the PI of a sample of cities, showing how Navojoa is more compact than Acapulco. *Less sprawling cities have higher PI values.*

5. **Clustering index.** In addition to measuring the overall shape of the city, the concept of compactness includes consideration of how concentrated people and employment are within the larger space. A CLI is used to measure the unequal distribution of jobs and people across a city. An extreme case would be one in which all people live in one census tract, and the other extreme would be a city where all census tracts have an equal number of residents. We calculate this index in a similar way to that of a location quotient, inspired in this respect

Map B.2 Maps Identifying the Equal Area Circles of Aguascalientes and Acapulco

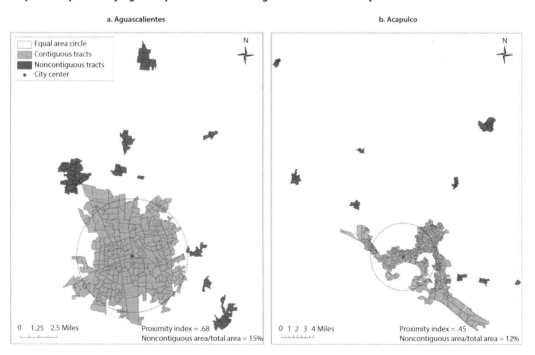

a. Aguascalientes

b. Acapulco

Equal area circle
Contiguous tracts
Noncontiguous tracts
• City center

0 1.25 2.5 Miles

Proximity index = .68
Noncontiguous area/total area = 15%

0 1 2 3 4 Miles

Proximity index = .45
Noncontiguous area/total area = 12%

Source: World Bank analysis based on population census data from the National Institute of Statistics and Geography (*Instituto Nacional de Estadística y Geografía*, INEGI).

by the work on urban centrality by Pereira et al. (2012). Thus, it takes the following form: $CLI = 1/2 \sum_{1}^{n} |s_i - 1/n|$, where n is the number of tracts in a city and s_i is the share of the city's population or employment in a given tract. In the 100 largest cities in Mexico, the CLI for population ranges from 0.21 to 0.64 and the average value is 0.36, whereas for jobs it ranges from 0.48 to 0.78 and has an average value of 0.58. Lower values indicate that people and jobs are more evenly spread out across the city. Not surprisingly, jobs are more clustered in space than housing. Figure B.7 compares the urban spatial form of Zacatecas-Guadalupe, where most population is clustered together in one contiguous urban area, and Queretaro, where a higher proportion of residents live in smaller clusters disconnected from the traditional urban center. *Less sprawling cities have higher CLI values.*

Figure B.6 Proximity Index Comparison, Selected Cities with Acapulco and Navojoa

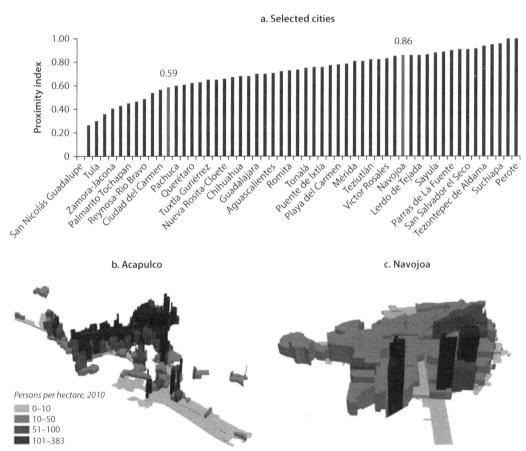

Source: World Bank analysis based on population census data from the National Institute of Statistics and Geography (*Instituto Nacional de Estadística y Geografía*, INEGI).

Figure B.7 Clustering Index Comparison, Selected Cities with Queretaro and Zacatecas-Guadalupe

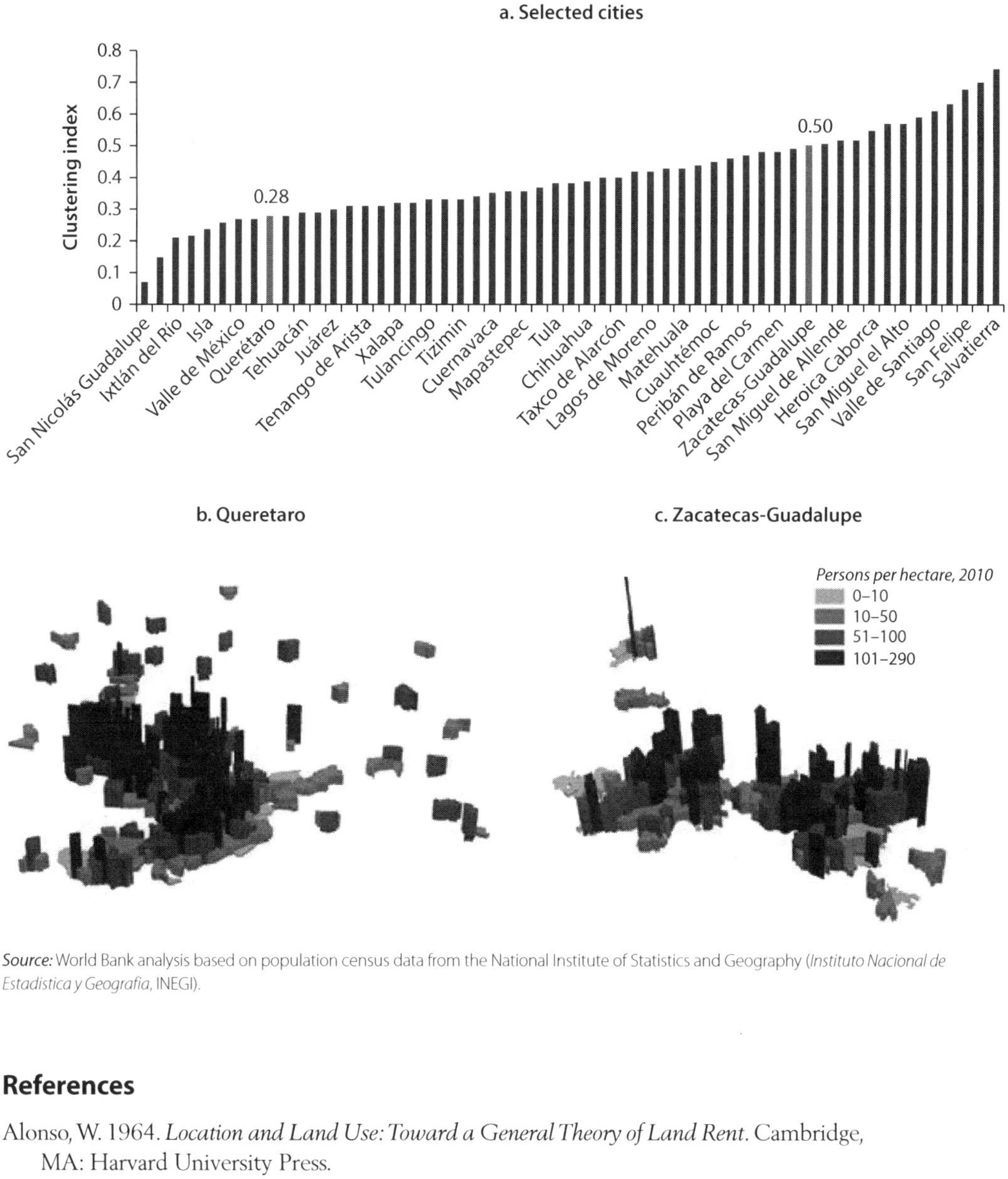

a. Selected cities

b. Queretaro

c. Zacatecas-Guadalupe

Persons per hectare, 2010
- 0–10
- 10–50
- 51–100
- 101–290

Source: World Bank analysis based on population census data from the National Institute of Statistics and Geography (*Instituto Nacional de Estadística y Geografía*, INEGI).

References

Alonso, W. 1964. *Location and Land Use: Toward a General Theory of Land Rent*. Cambridge, MA: Harvard University Press.

Angel, S., Jason Parent, and Daniel L. Civco. 2010. "The Fragmentation of Urban Footprints: Global Evidence of Sprawl, 1990–2000." LILP Working Paper, Lincoln Institute of Land Policy, Cambridge, MA.

Bertaud, A., and S. Malpezzi. 2003. "The Spatial Distribution of Population in 48 World Cities: Implications for Economies in Transition." Center for Urban Land Economics Research, University of Wisconsin, Madison.

Galster, G., R. Hanson, M. R. Ratcliffe, H. Wolman, S. Coleman, and J. Freihage. 2001. "Wrestling Sprawl to the Ground: Defining and Measuring an Elusive Concept." *Housing Policy Debate* 12 (4): 81–717.

Mills, E. S. 1967. "An Aggregative Model of Resource Allocation in a Metropolitan Area." *American Economic Review* 57 (2): 197–210.

Monkkonen, Paavo. 2008. "Using Online Satellite Imagery as a Research Tool: Mapping Changing Patterns of Urbanization in Mexico." *Journal of Planning Education and Research* 28 (2): 225–36.

Muth, R. F. 1969. *Cities and Housing: The Spatial Pattern of Urban Residential Land Use.* Chicago: University of Chicago Press.

Pereira, R. H. M., V. Nadalin, L. Monasterio, and P. H. M. Albuquerque. 2012. "Urban Centrality: A Simple Index." *Geographical Analysis* 45 (1): 77–89. doi:10.1111 /gean.12002.

Methodology for Case Study of Guadalajara Metropolitan Area

Introduction

Urban sprawl analyses using statistical measures are scarce in Mexico.[1] In Guadalajara, in particular, the analysis has been focused on the dynamics of the low-income population and informal settlements but without a comprehensive study considering all socioeconomic groups of the population (Schteingart 2001). The objective of the case study was to observe and analyze the relationship between urban sprawl, economic development, and the socioeconomic differences of different neighborhoods in the city to identify the main consequences of urban sprawl in terms of socioeconomic segregation. For the study, the Guadalajara Metropolitan Area was chosen for being one of biggest cities in Mexico that has experienced a significant urban expansion in the last years. A descriptive methodology of different variables was used for conducting the analysis using information of the Housing and Population Censuses, the Economic Censuses, the Income and Expenses Survey, the Origin and Destination Survey, and available information regarding air quality. This appendix presents in more detail the methodology and data sources used.

Definitions and Variables

Regions

The analysis of urban expansion and segregation within the Guadalajara Metropolitan Area uses only areas classified as urban because rural AGEBs (Basic Geostatistical Areas/Census Tracts, *Area Geoestadistica Básica*) and rural localities do not have enough information and in most of the cases are too small to be representative. In the case of localities, if an area has less than three households, the information is not provided by the Census to protect the population to be identified.

Information within the metropolitan area is aggregated at different levels of analysis. For example, housing information is provided at the postal code level, some of the census variables are available at the locality level, and some economic variables and the origin and destination survey are available at the AGEB level. It is not easy to homogenize the different levels of analysis because, for localities and postal codes, the geocoded information is provided as a point rather than a polygon. Then, it is not possible to know exactly the area limits.

In order to analyze different datasets (provided at AGEB, locality, or postal code levels), the information is aggregated by geographical location, splitting the whole urban region of the metropolitan area into nine different regions: center, north, south, east, west, northeast, northwest, southeast, and southwest. The extreme coordinates of the urban region are used to determine the limits of the metropolitan area, based on quadrants. Although the geographical area is the same for all regions, the number of localities and AGEBs is not homogeneous. For example, the northeast region takes only some localities and AGEBs of the municipality of Tonalá, but the rest of the region is not inside the metropolitan area of Guadalajara.

In total, the metropolitan area has 810 urban localities and 211 rural localities. In the northern side, there are only 24 localities, but one of these is the city of Guadalajara, the most populated region of the metropolitan area. In the maps below, the regions are identified with the AGEBs (map C.1), localities (map C.2), and postal codes (map C.3) that are considered in each region.

AGEBs

The first time the term AGEB was used in Mexico was in the Housing and Population Census of 1980. An AGEB, or a geographic and statistical area, is a territorial extension inside a municipality. There are urban AGEBs and rural AGEBs, depending on their housing density. An urban AGEB is a geographic area of a group of blocks delimited by streets, avenues, sidewalks, or other construction easily identified, in which its land is used mainly for occupational purposes, industries, provision of services, or commercial purposes. All urban AGEBs must be located inside urban localities.

An AGEB has three main attributes: (i) it is perfectly recognized in the terrain with identified topographic and durable characteristics; (ii) it has homogeneous geographic, economic, and social characteristics; and (iii) its extension is such that it could be covered by just one person (in order to conduct the interviews for the census).

The identification of the AGEBs changes every five years, depending on the changes a specific geographic area experienced. In 2000, the metropolitan area of Guadalajara had 1,278 urban AGEBs; this figure increased to 1,705 in 2010 (a growth of 33 percent, mainly located in the southern side, as shown in the analysis of the territorial expansion). Map C.1 shows the urban AGEBs by region in the Guadalajara Metropolitan Area.

Map C.1 Urban AGEBs by Region in the Guadalajara Metropolitan Area

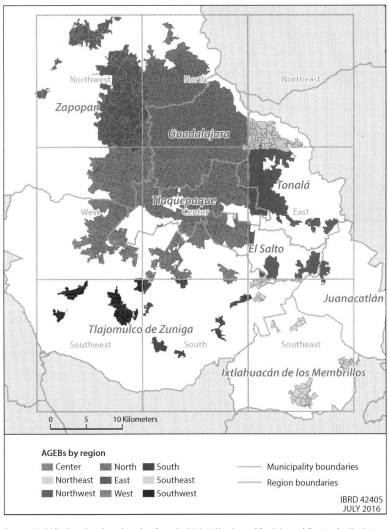

Source: World Bank analysis based on data from the National Institute of Statistics and Geography (*Instituto Nacional de Estadística y Geografía*, INEGI).
Note: AGEB = Basic Geostatistical Area/Census Tract (*Área Geoestadística Básica*).

Locations

An urban locality is identified as an area with a population of 2,500 inhabitants or more, or the main municipality of a state, regardless of the number of inhabitants. The localities are not as changeable as the AGEBs, so their comparison through different years is more stable. Localities are also classified as urban and rural depending on the land use. However, urban localities are very small (in terms of territory), so the number of localities in rural areas grows exponentially when compared to urban localities. For example, the municipality of Guadalajara, which is the main municipality in the metropolitan area in terms of population, has four localities, whereas the municipality of Tlajomulco de Zúñiga, with a population of only 416 thousand, has 309 localities.

For this analysis, only urban localities are considered. As of 2010, the metropolitan area of Guadalajara has 819 urban localities and 211 rural localities. Map C.2 shows the urban localities by region in the Guadalajara Metropolitan Area.

Map C.2 Localities by Region in the Guadalajara Metropolitan Area

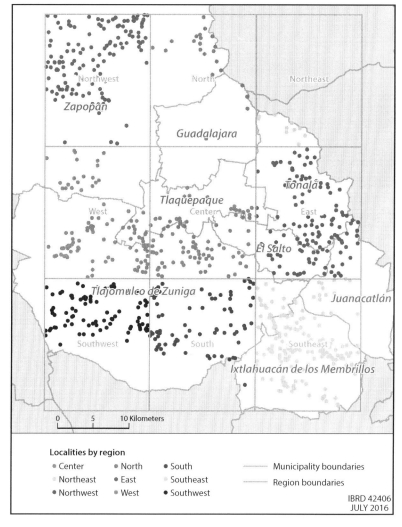

Source: World Bank analysis based on data from the National Institute of Statistics and Geography (*Instituto Nacional de Estadística y Geografía*, INEGI).

Postal Codes

The National Postal Code Catalogue is provided by the Mexican postal service. The National Institute of Statistics and Geography (*Instituto Nacional de Estadística y Geografía*, INEGI) uses mainly information of localities and AGEBs, but the Federal Mortgage Society (*Sociedad Hipotecaria Federal*, SHF) provides housing information (assessments and housing characteristics) geocoded at the postal code level. Table C.1 shows the number of postal codes by municipality in the metropolitan area and map C.3 illustrates their location by region. Not all the postal codes have housing information, since most of them correspond to rural areas in which the Federal Mortgage Society does not report any activity.

Detailed Methodology and Results of Analysis

Housing

The main source for the analysis of housing information came from SHF. Data provided by SHF is reported at the individual level, but the lowest level of specific location of the properties is postal code level. Although there are 1,959 postal codes in the metropolitan area of Guadalajara, housing information for 2010 is available only for 331 postal codes distributed among the nine regions as shown in table C.2.

SHF collects an official appraisal for each property as a collateral-backed mortgage granted by financial intermediaries. The appraisal is performed based on at least six transactions involving similar properties in the local market. The data cover six years from January 2008 to December 2013, and observations are geocoded at the postal code level. The dataset includes the unit appraisal (which would be the proxy for price) and some dwelling characteristics such as size of the plot, built-up area, the type of dwelling (house, apartment, or house in a gated community), urban proximity to the city center, number of bedrooms, number of bathrooms, number of stories, number of parking spaces, age of the property, and some characteristics related to the public services of

Table C.1 Total Number of Postal Codes by Region

Municipality	Number of postal codes
Guadalajara	453
Ixtlahuacán de los Membrillos	14
Juanacatlán	9
El Salto	67
Tlajomulco de Zúñiga	231
Tlaquepaque	247
Tonalá	345
Zapopan	593
Total	1,959

Source: National Postal Code Catalogue, http://www.geopostcodes.com.

Map C.3 Postal Codes by Region in the Guadalajara Metropolitan Area

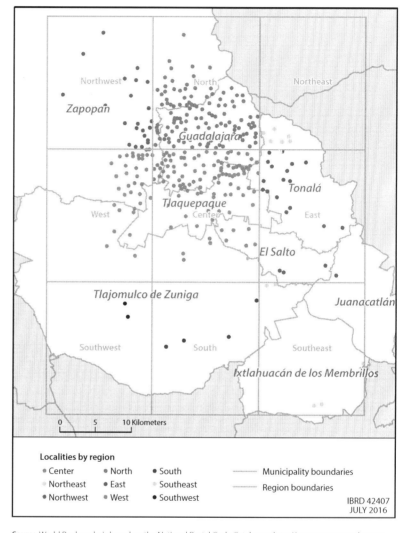

Source: World Bank analysis based on the National Postal Code Catalogue, http://www.geopostcodes.com.

the neighborhood. The number of observations for the metropolitan area of Guadalajara for the six years is 172,030.

For conducting the analysis, the information was aggregated for each region (taking the median assessment value and the average information per each region) and calculating the trends. The number of housing observations per each region is shown in table C.3.

We can observe from the table above that the number of observations is similar in every year, meaning that this dataset is not capturing the properties' growth within each region during the five years of study. However, the dataset provides information of the evolution of the assessment values from 2008 to 2013, as well as changes in the characteristics of properties sold every year.

Table C.2 Number of Postal Codes by Region with Housing Information

Geographical location	Postal codes
Center	114
North	120
Northeast	6
Northwest	23
East	22
South	5
Southeast	4
Southwest	2
West	37
Total	331

Source: Information regarding the location of properties obtained from the Federal Mortgage Society (*Sociedad Hipotecaria Federal*, SHF).

Table C.3 Number of Housing Observations (and Postal Codes with Observation) per Region and Year, 2008–13

Geographical location	Number of observations by year (Number of postal codes with observations each year)					
	2008	2009	2010	2011	2012	2013
Center	16,174 (100)	16,141 (90)	16,169 (97)	16,161 (98)	16,172 (101)	16,157 (100)
North	3,957 (107)	3,946 (102)	3,950 (105)	3,926 (100)	3,958 (106)	3,953 (108)
Northeast	796 (5)	722 (3)	792 (4)	796 (5)	803 (6)	803 (6)
Northwest	6,474 (21)	6,474 (21)	6,474 (21)	6,474 (21)	6,471 (20)	6,474 (21)
East	5,449 (15)	5,933 (17)	6,096 (18)	6,096 (18)	6,096 (18)	6,090 (17)
South	2,153 (2)	2,153 (2)	2,153 (2)	2,153 (2)	2,153 (2)	5,672 (2)
Southeast	517 (3)	517 (3)	517 (3)	517 (3)	517 (3)	517 (3)
Southwest	9,190 (2)	9,190 (2)	9,190 (2)	9,190 (2)	9,190 (2)	9,190 (2)
West	5,663 (33)	5,669 (34)	5,671 (34)	5,671 (34)	5,666 (35)	5,672 (35)
Total	50,373 (288)	50,745 (274)	51,012 (286)	50,984 (283)	51,026 (293)	51,009 (294)

Source: Housing information obtained from the Federal Mortgage Society (*Sociedad Hipotecaria Federal*, SHF).

In addition to SHF, analysis on housing conditions in the Guadalajara Metropolitan Area was carried out drawing from the 2012 Socioeconomic Conditions Module of the Income and Expenses Survey. Although the survey was conducted also in 2008 and 2010, only the survey of 2012 included information at the AGEB level allowing us to analyze the information by regions within the metropolitan area of Guadalajara. The Socioeconomic Conditions Module includes questions asked at the housing level, individual level, and household level, and the information relevant for this section was taken from the different questionnaires conducted at the different levels. The survey did not include any AGEB located in the south or southeast of the city. Therefore, for the analysis of the southern part, information is available only for the southwest. With this data, we analyzed how much households in different parts of the city spend in mortgage or rent and housing conditions and formality (in terms of tenure, tenure documents, and access to formal mortgage credit).

Urban Infrastructure and Amenities

INEGI calculates an index from 1 to 4 in which each area is categorized depending on its level of urban equipment. The urban equipment is defined as those areas in which extracurricular activities are taking place, or places that offer social welfare services to the population or support to economic activities. SHF calculates a ratio surrounding the property and evaluates the urban equipment within this diameter: churches, markets, public squares, parks and gardens, schools, hospitals, and public transport stations (urban or suburban).

According to SHF, the urban equipment index is calculated by defining a ratio of 2 kilometers surrounding the property and observing the different urban facilities in this parameter. Four levels of urban equipment are defined as follows:

1. When the area of the parameter does not have equipment described in number 2
2. When the area of the parameter has a church, a market or several stores, schools, parks and gardens
3. When the area of the parameter has the facilities described in number 2 plus accessibility to a public transport station
4. When the area of the parameter has the facilities described in 3 plus hospitals and banks.

Accessibility to Public Transport

In terms of accessibility, we analyze how far away or close by (at the median) the properties in each region are. Properties are geocoded at the postal code level, so the distance measures are just an approximation of how far the properties are from public transportation. Guadalajara has two massive public transportation projects. The first one is called the *Tren Ligero* or light rail train (LRT) that has two lines: one crossing the city from north to south and one crossing the city from east to west. The LRT also has feeder buses called *Pretren* (with only one line implemented in January 2007). The second transport system, the bus rapid transit (BRT) line called *Macrobus*, was inaugurated on March 2009 (the LRT was functioning during the six years of analysis with data). The *Macrobus* line provides service to the municipalities of Tlajomulco de Zúñiga and El Salto.

Table C.4 Median Distance in Meters for the Closest Macrobus and LRT Stations for Each Region

Region	Distance to the closest Macrobus station (median in meters)	Distance to the closest LRT station (median in meters)
Center	8,722.35	8,665.80
Northeast	9,163.56	3,585.66
Northwest	18,997.53	15,579.50
North	4,599.04	3,248.57
East	11,811.06	5,718.72
West	12,174.23	7,180.37
South	19,727.93	21,528.21
Southeast	15,120.86	18,221.06
Southwest	18,694.38	15,849.63

Source: Distances calculated by the World Bank using information from the Federal Mortgage Society (*Sociedad Hipotecaria Federal*, SHF) and location of transport stations.
Note: LRT = light rail train.

Given that the two public transport systems provide services to and from Guadalajara's downtown, which is located in the city of Guadalajara, the regions of the metropolitan area with the best public transport accessibility are the northern and central regions. Table C.4 shows the median distance in meters from the closest public transport station (*Macrobus* and LRT) for every region analyzed.

Commuting Times and Mobility

The analysis of commuting times and mobility is based on data from the 2009 National Survey about the Use of Time in Mexico (*Encuesta Nacional sobre Uso del Tiempo*, ENUT), the 2008 Origin and Destination Survey for the Guadalajara Metropolitan Area, and the 2012 Socioeconomic Conditions Module of the Income and Expenses Survey. It is important to note that the 2009 ENUT provides data only at the municipality level and does not include all municipalities in the Guadalajara Metropolitan Area. The 2009 ENUT only asked how much work commuting time the individuals spend per week. In contrast, the 2008 Origin and Destination Survey also includes information on how much time and money households spend on their commuting trips daily.

The 2008 Origin and Destination Survey was conducted by the *Centro Estatal de Investigación de la Viabilidad y el Transporte*, using a survey design based on random stratified sample by clusters. Although the housing units were selected in each AGEB, the survey is representative only for the metropolitan area of Guadalajara but not for each AGEB. However, by aggregating the AGEBs by region, we ended up analyzing a fair number of observations in each area, allowing us to draw some conclusions about commuting time and expenses for the whole metropolitan area.

The survey was conducted in different locations. Most of the information included in this section belongs to the questionnaires raised to individuals at home asking them about the different trips conducted the day before. However, some of the questions were taken also from the questionnaires asked in different companies of their employees. Although the survey provides information about every trip made in a regular day, the analysis in this section is focused mainly on the first trip, from home to a specific destination.

Some of the questions included in the Socioeconomic Conditions Module of the Income and Expenses Survey also relate to mobility, including the number of cars owned in each household, the commuting experience of employees in different companies, and the distance from their home to the nearest hospital.

Socioeconomic Disparities

ITER (what INEGI calls the "main results by locality") variables provide Housing and Population Census information at the locality level and are used twice in this analysis: first, to analyze some of the sociodemographic characteristics of individuals in each of the localities in Guadalajara, namely education, economic indicators, wage structure, and demographic trends; and, second, when analyzing the CONEVAL (National Council for the Evaluation of Social Development Policy [*Consejo Nacional de Evaluación de la Política de Desarrollo Social*]) segregation index, which is based on housing infrastructure. It is important to note that not all variables are available for every year; in this case, the analysis was conducted with the available information.

The number of localities per each municipality of the metropolitan area of Guadalajara is shown in table C.5.

Of 1,030 localities in Guadalajara, 819 are urban localities, and these are the ones that would be considered in the ITER analysis, as shown in table C.6.

The northern side has only 24 localities, but the main locality of the city of Guadalajara is located in this area. Conversely, there are 132 localities in the northwest and 135 localities in the east corresponding to the municipality of Zapopan and Tonalá.

Table C.5　Number of Localities per Municipality

Municipality	Number of localities per municipality	% of total localities
El Salto	52	6.3
Guadalajara	4	0.5
Ixtlahuacán de los Membrillos	135	16.5
Juanacatlán	35	4.3
Tlajomulco de Zúñiga	309	37.7
Tlaquepaque	36	4.4
Tonalá	76	9.3
Zapopan	172	21
Total	819	100

Source: Main results by locality (ITER) provided by the National Institute of Statistics and Geography (*Instituto Nacional de Estadística y Geografía*, INEGI).

Table C.6 Number of Urban Localities per Region

Region	Number of localities per region	% of total
Center	87	10.62
Northeast	10	1.22
Northwest	132	16.12
North	24	2.93
East	135	16.48
West	101	12.33
South	73	8.91
Southeast	170	20.76
Southwest	87	1.62
Total	819	100

Source: World Bank categorization of localities per region based on main results by locality (ITER) provided by the National Institute of Statistics and Geography (*Instituto Nacional de Estadística y Geografía*, INEGI).

In addition to income poverty, CONEVAL calculates the *social lag index*. The social lag index is calculated using a principal component methodology that combines indicators regarding different public goods and services shortages in each of the households in Mexico. Whereas the income poverty is calculated only at the municipality, state, and national levels, the social lag index is also calculated at the locality level.

The variables considered for the calculation of the index are the following:

- Percentage of illiterate adults (15 years old and older) over the total number of adults
- Percentage of the population between 6 and 14 years old who do not attend school
- Percentage of households with population between 15 and 29 years old with a member who achieved fewer than 9 schooling years
- Percentage of the adult population with incomplete primary school
- Percentage of population with no access to health services
- Percentage of occupied properties with inadequate floors
- Percentage of properties with no toilet
- Percentage of properties without official water services (connection to public service)
- Percentage of properties without sewerage
- Percentage of properties without electricity
- Percentage of properties without washing machine or refrigerator

Once the index is calculated, using a weighted sum of each indicator, the results were classified in five categories: very low, low, medium, high, and very high, where localities classified as "very low" have very low levels of social lag (or segregation), whereas localities classified as "very high" have higher segregation problems and a very high social lag index. This latter classification is based on the index for every locality in Mexico (national level, not just the metropolitan area).

Economic Opportunities

The analysis of economic opportunities within the Guadalajara Metropolitan Area was based on the Socioeconomic Conditions Module of the Survey of Income and Expenses. This module includes questions on the hours, income, and conditions of work.

Although the module does not explicitly ask whether individuals have informal or formal jobs, two questions regarding the conditions at work may indicate the existence of informality: whether employees contribute to social security or whether they have or do not have a job contract.

We classify the number of hours worked the week and month before the survey was conducted in three different categories, relative to the general distribution of hours worked for the whole metropolitan area: in the first category are individuals who work hours below the 25th percentile of the distribution for the metropolitan region; in the second category are individuals who worked hours between the 25th percentile and the 75th percentile of the distribution; and in the last group are individuals who worked hours above the 75th percentile of the distribution.

Similarly, the analyses of the three-month income and the current income by region were conducted by defining three income categories based on an observation of the overall income distribution for the Guadalajara Metropolitan Area: less than 25th percentile, between the 25th percentile and the 75th percentile, and more than 75th percentile.

Environmental Implications

Information about the differential environmental effects in the metropolitan area of Guadalajara were taken from the Monitoring Atmospheric System of Jalisco which calculates the Air Quality Metropolitan Index (IMECA) in ten different stations in the metropolitan area (there were only eight stations in 2000).

Note

1. An exception is observed for Mexico City that has been studied extensively, not only through its territorial expansion but also through the population distribution and segregation.

Reference

Schteingart, M. 2001. "La División Social del Espacio en las Ciudades." *Perfiles Latinoamericanos* 10: 13–31.

Environmental Benefits Statement

The World Bank Group is committed to reducing its environmental footprint. In support of this commitment, World Bank Publications leverages electronic publishing options and print-on-demand technology, which is located in regional hubs worldwide. Together, these initiatives enable print runs to be lowered and shipping distances decreased, resulting in reduced paper consumption, chemical use, greenhouse gas emissions, and waste.

World Bank Publications follows the recommended standards for paper use set by the Green Press Initiative. The majority of our books are printed on Forest Stewardship Council (FSC)–certified paper, with nearly all containing 50–100 percent recycled content. The recycled fiber in our book paper is either unbleached or bleached using totally chlorine-free (TCF), processed chlorine-free (PCF), or enhanced elemental chlorine-free (EECF) processes.

More information about the Bank's environmental philosophy can be found at http://www.worldbank.org/corporateresponsibility.